P9-DBY-425

ALSO BY THOMAS GILOVICH

How We Know What Isn't So: The Fallibility of Human Reason in Everyday Life

Why Smart People Make Big Money Mistakes—and How to Correct Them

LESSONS FROM THE NEW SCIENCE OF BEHAVIORAL ECONOMICS

GARY BELSKY
AND THOMAS GILOVICH

SIMON & SCHUSTER PAPERBACKS
NEW YORK LONDON TORONTO SYDNEY

SIMON & SCHUSTER PAPERBACKS
Rockefeller Center
1230 Avenue of the Americas
New York, NY 10020

For information about special discounts for bulk purchases,
please contact Simon & Schuster Special Sales:
1-800-456-6798 or business@simonandschuster.com.

Manufactured in the United States of America

10

The Library of Congress has cataloged the hardcover edition as follows:
Belsky, Gary.
Why smart people make big money mistakes—and how
to correct them : lessons from the new science
of behavioral economics / Gary Belsky and Thomas Gilovich.
p. cm.
1. Finance, Personal—Psychological aspects.
2. Finance, Personal—Decision making. 3. Investments—Decision making.
4. Consumers—Attitudes. 5. Economics—Psychological aspects.
I. Gilovich, Thomas. II. Title.
HG179.B375 1999
332.024—dc21 98-31145 CIP
ISBN 0-684-84493-1
0-684-85938-6 (Pbk)

G.B.:
To my mom, Irene Chervitz Belsky, and to my dad, Morris Belsky, of blessed memory.

T.G.:
To Karen, Ilana, and Rebecca

CONTENTS

INTRODUCTION

WHY SMART PEOPLE MAKE BIG MONEY MISTAKES

This is an optimistic book, written by a pair of realists. Optimistic, because this volume rests on the belief that ordinary individuals can enhance their enjoyment of life by understanding—and altering—the way they deal with their money. Realistic, because your authors know that correcting money-related behavior is a lot like tinkering with a golf swing or getting along better with in-laws: it may take a while, and for every remedy there's always the danger that you will create a whole new set of problems. Still, our purpose here is straightforward, and we are confident of its merits. We believe that by identifying the psychological causes behind many types of financial decisions, you can effectively change your behavior in ways that will ultimately put more money in your pocket and help you keep more of what you already have.

How do we plan to conjure up this remarkable transformation? The insights and strategies we offer arise from a variety of well-springs, not least among them our own experiences as a psychologist and as a journalist specializing in personal finance. We're also spenders, savers, and investors much like yourself, possessing firsthand knowledge of the money mistakes we'll be discussing. Underpinning most of this book, however, is a field of research that has flourished on college campuses and in other intellectual arenas for the better part of three decades, but one that until now has never had a proper airing in the popular media. This area of inquiry is sometimes referred to as "behavioral finance," but we call it "behavioral economics." Behavioral economics combines the twin disciplines of psychology and economics to explain why and how people make seemingly irrational or illogical decisions when they spend, invest, save, and borrow money.

Why, in other words, do smart people make big money mistakes?

As you're probably aware, confusion about money—how we earn it, how we spend it, how we waste it—may be more prevalent today than at any period in this country's history. From IRAs to 401(k)s to CMOs, most Americans are overwhelmed by the alphabet soup of financial information, lingo, and options that are now common to our daily existence. This deluge of new opportunities (and perils) has only added to the widespread befuddlement that has long plagued most of us when it comes to the choices we make at the car dealer, department store, or bank. Indeed, whether in the stock market, the real estate market, or the supermarket, we all commit financial follies that cost us hundreds or thousands of dollars every year. Yet in the main, we are blissfully ignorant of the causes of most of our monetary missteps and clueless as to how we might correct them.

- Why, for example, do so many investors sell stocks just *before* the share prices skyrocket? And why do those same investors keep a tight grip on lousy stocks until they plummet to the earth?
- Why do mutual fund investors put their money into the latest "hot" funds, when those same portfolios routinely lag behind the overall stock or bond markets?
- Why do so many Americans stash their money in passbook savings accounts or bank CDs when they're actually losing money by doing so?
- Why are so many of us willing to spend so much more for a product bought on credit than with cash?
- Why do business executives spend ever-increasing amounts of money on failing products or money-losing corporate divisions?
- Why are most workers happier with a 10 percent raise when the inflation rate is 12 percent than with a 3 percent raise when inflation is at 4 percent? And why is that bad?
- Why do so many people have such low deductibles on their insurance policies?

The answers to these pervasive and puzzling questions can be found in behavioral economics. But before we throw you headfirst into this unusual science, allow us to take you on a quick tour of its history. By examining how economics came to be linked with psychology (in academia, that is; they've always been linked in real life), you'll be that much better prepared to grasp how behavioral economics can help improve your finances.

A (MERCIFULLY) BRIEF HISTORY OF ECONOMICS

There's an old joke that if you laid every economist in history end to end, they still wouldn't reach a conclusion. But in fact, economists have been describing the way money and mankind interact for quite a while, often with impressive (if dubious) certainty. In 1848, for instance, British economist and philosopher John Stuart Mill wrote in his *Principles of Political Economy:* "Happily, there is nothing in the laws of value which remains for the present or any future writer to clear up; the theory of the subject is complete." Mill's forecast notwithstanding, the study of economics has continued to draw some of the world's greatest minds, individuals who have developed a variety of theories to explain how people (and groups of people, such as companies and countries) go about the business of allocating available resources to achieve desired goals. These thinkers have ranged from the fourth-century (B.C.) Greek philosopher Plato (who was one of the first to recognize the economic basis of social life) to the renowned eighteenth-century Scotsman Adam Smith (one of the first to systematically explore the nature of economic markets) to the twentieth-century Englishman John Maynard Keynes (who revolutionized the way we look at the economy as a whole).

Whatever the prevailing theory, economic study has traditionally been informed by a few core beliefs or assumptions. The most significant assumption is that humans are fundamentally rational and ultimately efficient when it comes to money. Put simply: We know what we want, what we want is for our own good, and we know (or will eventually figure out) the best way to get it. In short, people make rational, consistent, and self-interested decisions.

But of course, while most people are self-interested, very few are consistent, and even fewer are perfectly rational. What is consistent or rational, for example, about the person who thinks saving $5 is sufficiently worthwhile to drive twenty minutes to a discount grocery store, but who throws away hundreds of dollars a year on the gas-guzzling car used for the trip? On the other hand, where's the self-interest in giving money to charity or taking a friend out to dinner? To be fair, economists don't confuse self-interest with selfishness. Most economic models assume that people can find value in things that do not necessarily increase or enhance their material well-being. They concede that humans can be motivated by nonfinancial concerns such as love or generosity or convenience.

Nonetheless, the notion of rational and consistent self-interest requires a belief that people donate to the United Way, buy a Honda, or invest in Microsoft based on a consistent calculation of value. That is, we assign a value to the good feeling that generosity brings—as well as to the loss of buying power or investing power that donating money entails—and we make decisions accordingly. To be sure, economic theory acknowledges that these calculations are not always made on a conscious level. But it is a fundamental truth of conventional economics that such an evaluation of benefits and costs exists, if only on a subconscious and experiential plane. On one level or another, traditional theory insists, we make the decisions we make because of a consistent and rational pursuit of satisfaction and personal fulfillment, of getting the most out of life with our current and future resources.

As you might imagine, such a dogged insistence on rationality, self-interest, and consistency as the driving forces behind financial decisions has often put economists in a quandary: how to explain seemingly irrational human behavior as a function of self-interest. Consider, as just one example, our habit of tipping. If you think about it, tipping is about as irrational as can be: folks routinely giving away money without a clear obligation to do so, to people they'll likely never see again, in places they'll never revisit, for a level of service that may not have even pleased them. According to a 1996 survey by Market Facts of Arlington Heights, Illinois, 94 percent of Americans who have the occasion to tip food servers always or usually do so.

Hardly surprising, right? Everybody tips because, well, we just do. For economists, though, explaining why people tip has always been a tough chore. It's not enough to say that the self-interest in tipping is the guarantee of good service. Since tipping comes *after* the meal, that would only explain why people might tip in neighborhood restaurants or other eateries to which they are certain they will return. It does not explain why travelers tip the waiter at a Denny's in, say, Little Rock, when they know it is unlikely they will ever eat there again. Where's the self-interest in that? Nor is it sufficient to explain tipping as simply the result of goodwill—a heartwarming calculation by the vast majority of Americans that results in the conclusion that being nice to service people is worth about 15 percent of whatever we spend. If that were the case, we'd all be tipping gas station attendants, cashiers, and bank tellers.

So why do Americans tip? No one knows for certain, but Russell Roberts, an economist at Washington University in St. Louis, has some interesting thoughts on the matter. He notes that people frequently use social rules of thumb when interacting with each other, without conscious acknowledgment, as a way to make life a more pleasant experience. For example, most of us agree to wait our turn in line at the car wash rather than bang fenders with one another to get there first. Roberts theorizes that Americans have an unspoken rule of thumb about dining at restaurants: We all want to eat out, and we all want the experience to be pleasant (if being served cold food by a grouch was the goal, we could just stay home). So because diners themselves can better ensure good service than restaurant managers, a social rule of thumb evolved at some point that servers would be paid low wages that would be supplemented by tips. Problem solved. Restaurant managers leave the difficult job of policing their staff to patrons—allegedly, the word "tip" has its origins in eighteenth-century England, where coffeehouse patrons were asked to put coins in a box labeled "To Insure Promptness." The problem today, of course, is that many people tip without thinking. According to one survey, only 54 percent of respondents said they based their tip on the quality of service; 30 percent tip out of pity; and roughly 10 percent say they tip because it's expected. That's why the next time you have lousy service at a restaurant, don't blame the server—blame previous customers who didn't uphold their end of the social contract by refusing to tip when the service was poor.

Whether you agree with Roberts's theory or not, the tipping mystery is just a minor demonstration of how economists have found it difficult to integrate into their assumptions of rationality, self-interest, and consistency those aspects of human behavior that most mortals would identify as central to money decisions: things like guilt, fear, regret, compulsiveness, addiction, bad habits, ego, and peer pressure, to name just a few. There's no little irony in the inability of most of history's greatest economic minds to recognize the influence of commonplace human characteristics on money decisions, given that most businesses exploit these frailties as a matter of course. The modern fashion industry, for example, rests almost solely upon the public's seemingly irrational willingness to pay more than they would otherwise need to clothe themselves for items whose only discernible appeal is that very skinny, very pale people look good wearing them. Similarly, economic theory was essentially at a loss—even if economists wouldn't admit it—to explain why people stampede to invest in the stock of companies for no better reason than that other investors were doing the same.

Why, traditional economics has been pained to explain, do people routinely make decisions that are not rational, self-interested, or consistent? Answering that question is essential to the task of trying to help people utilize their resources more efficiently—that is, to get more bang for their buck.

The solution, or at least the firm beginnings of a solution, began to crystallize some thirty years ago, when a new breed of researchers took on the task. Many of these newcomers were psychologists, not economists. They were the pioneers of behavioral economics. As is the case with many achievements of broad scope, it's difficult to pin medals for the creation of behavioral economics on one or two chests, but we suspect we'll get little argument if we begin the telling of this tale at Hebrew University in Jerusalem, Israel, in the late 1960s. There, two psychologists—Amos Tversky and Daniel Kahneman—were discussing the way Israeli aviation instructors had been motivating their pilots in training. The flight instructors, who were taking a class that Kahneman taught at Hebrew U., argued against the conventional wisdom that rewards were a more effective teaching tool than punishments. Rather, the officers found that when a pilot was praised for a good flight he tended to do worse the next time in the air, while pilots who were criticized after a poor performance routinely did better the next time they flew.

Readers familiar with statistics probably recognize the flaw in the officers' conclusion and in their theory of motivation. In the nineteenth century, a British scientist named Sir Francis Galton introduced a concept called "statistical regression." He explained how in any series of uncertain events that tend to fall around an average or mean—imagine taking two dozen swings at a tennis ball, for instance—any extraordinary single event will likely be followed by one that is closer to average. So a really bad forehand will generally be followed by one that is slightly better, and a really great backhand will likely be followed by one that isn't so crisp. That's the nature of probabilistic events, and it's why exceptionally tall people tend to have children who are not as tall and why exceptionally short people tend to have children who are not quite so short. Kahneman recognized that any single performance by a pilot—good or bad—would likely have been followed by a flight that moved closer, or regressed, to that pilot's long-term average. So the pilots who were criticized for a poor flight were more likely to do better the next time *regardless* of what their instructors did, while those who had received compliments were statistically more likely to do worse on their next flight. Not knowing this, the officers had concluded that the criticism was helping their pilots perform better and the praise was somehow making their performance suffer.

Although Kahneman pointed out the flaw to the officers—presumably enhancing the self-esteem of future generations of Israeli fighter pilots!—the real significance of this episode was that it prompted him and Tversky to begin thinking more about human judgment and decision making in various arenas of life. What was remarkable about the flight instructors' experience was that events seemed to conspire against the correct conclusion. Subpar flights *did* tend to follow praise, and superior flights *did* tend to follow criticism. And unless a flight instructor knew about regression ahead of time, the only logical conclusion was that punishment worked and rewards didn't. In what other areas of life, the two psychologists wondered, were the proper conclusions hard to see because of faulty intuitions or the fiendishly complicated nature of the information available? Tversky seized upon one such instance and put it to work in one of the classic experiments on human judgment. Take the test yourself:

Imagine that two bags are filled—out of your sight—with the same number of poker chips. In one bag, two-thirds of the chips are red and the remainder are white. In the other bag, the proportions are reversed

—one-third of the chips are red and the remaining two-thirds are white. Your task is to guess which is the bag with mostly red chips and which is the bag with mostly white chips. You're asked to grab a handful from bag A—say, five chips—and many handfuls from bag B—say, thirty chips. As it happens, four of the five chips you pulled from bag A are red, while twenty of the thirty chips you pulled from bag B are red. Which bag would you guess has more red chips?

If you're like most people, you probably reasoned that bag A has the most red chips because 80 percent (four out of five) of the chips you picked were red, while in bag B a less convincing 66 percent (twenty out of thirty) of those you chose were red. But you would have been more justified in your answer if you had guessed bag B. Reason: Statistics tells us that the larger the sample (thirty chips versus five), the more reliable the conclusion or outcome.

All well and good, but what, you might ask, does this have to do with economics or the way people handle their money? Quite a lot, actually. Consider how often people make decisions in life based on small, statistically insignificant or inconclusive samples—say, an investor in Boston who sees a long line at a new fast-food chain and decides to buy the company's newly issued stock, only to discover when the stock's price falls that the lines in Boston were the result of poor service, which resulted in many customers deciding not to return. Or an investor who buys a mutual fund because it beat the market over the past year—and then finds herself owning a fund that goes on to underperform the average.

Beyond this, Tversky and Kahneman's experiments were important from an economic point of view because they made it clear that people's judgments and decisions are not always fully rational. While this may seem as earth-shattering as proving that the sun rises in the morning, the act of scientifically validating what seems to be common sense was in this case quite significant, for several reasons. Not the least was that Kahneman and Tversky (and many others who followed) were able to start describing and classifying many of the particular tricks that people use to simplify and solve some of the difficult problems of judgment and choice that confront them. Kahneman and Tversky referred to these simplifying procedures as "judgmental heuristics"—mental shortcuts (or rules of thumb) that most people rely on reflexively. Such guidelines might be instinctive (a long line at a restaurant probably means business is good) or societally reinforced (it's a good idea to stretch your budget when buying a house), but in either case they are sometimes misleading. Long lines at a restaurant can mean that the service is slow or that other competing restaurants are closed, and home prices don't rise as fast or as much as Americans think, which means there is frequently no financial justification for buying more house than you can afford in the hope that price hikes will reward you later.

As Tversky and Kahneman were joined by other researchers—psychologists and economists—they essentially created the body of work that we place under the rubric of behavioral economics. The two Israelis, by the way, eventually migrated to the United States and became ambassadors of behavioral economics—Kahneman from his current perch at Princeton University in New Jersey, and Tversky at Stanford University in Palo Alto, California. Sadly, Tversky died of cancer in 1996 at age fifty-nine. Tversky, who earned Israel's highest honor for bravery during his military career, once said that all he really did was use scientific methods to explore aspects of human behavior that were already known to "advertisers and used-car salesmen." In reality, behavioral economics has become a significant force in both academia and business—even in national economic policy. Not too long ago, for instance, University of Chicago behavioral economist Richard Thaler—one of the leading lights in the field—testified before the Senate Finance Committee about savings habits in the United States. Thaler explained how "mental accounting"—a subject we'll cover in chapter 1—contributes to the low rate of savings in this country (around 4 percent, vs. better than 15 percent in Japan, for example).

Still, there's one realm where behavioral economics has yet to achieve prominence, and it may be the most important: in the minds of typical consumers, borrowers, savers, spenders, and investors. That's who this book is for. We've distilled three decades of academic research—the labors of Kahneman, Tversky, and dozens of others, including one of your authors—into an easy-to-navigate guide to the workings of our money mind-sets.

THE METHOD TO OUR MADNESS

Like many endeavors, the writing of this book posed a variety of interesting problems. Some were small, such as how to refer to ourselves in a book whose tone is meant to be that of a conversation at a cocktail party. That's easy when we're a unified front—"We hope you recommend this book to lots of people"—but more difficult when the voice is specific to one or the other of us: "I'm a professor of psychology at Cornell University" is something only Tom could say honestly, while Gary alone would be correct in noting, "I was a writer at *Money* magazine." This is an important issue, since we bring our individual experiences to the table for your edification—the anecdotes we'll use to highlight poor decision making come from real life—and it strikes us as misleading to use the phrase "a friend of ours" or "someone we know" when only one of us knows the person in question. Our solution, then, is to refer to ourselves in the third person when appropriate, as in "This solution was Gary's idea." Forgive us, on such occasions, if we sound like self-absorbed rock stars.

We also worried about expectations, specifically the presumptions of readers who may have come to expect a certain tone and approach from the seemingly endless stream of self-help guides that are now ubiquitous in bookstores. So, for the record: We have tried to avoid the trappings of most pop psychology books. That is, despite the fact that Tom is a psychologist, there will be no attempt between these covers to psychoanalyze *you.* There will be no theorizing, for example, that a tendency to rack up staggering Visa card balances is the result of having been breast-fed for too long or too briefly, or that the impulse is in your genes. There will be no attempts, moreover, to identify an inner child, inner investor, or pretty much inner anything. That's not to say we oppose these sorts of books out of hand (some no doubt give succor to their readers).

But to the extent that you seek to discover some Freudian cause of your individual psychological tendencies with regard to money, you'll find our "virtual couch" wanting. Although we expect to help you avoid getting into debt by showing how credit cards cheapen money—to cite just one example in this book—we have little hope of illuminating the reason that you *in particular* fall prey to that tendency. Our focus in this book is on patterns of thought and behavior that lead most people—people *in general*—to get less out of their financial choices than they should.

That focus is not always easy to maintain, in part because some fundamental concepts of behavioral economics can appear to contradict each other at times. This is not surprising, given the way the human mind works. But we don't want readers of one chapter to throw up their hands in dismay when the next chapter seems to be saying something quite opposite. An example? In chapter 7 we'll talk about herding, which is the tendency many people have to rely too much on the opinions or actions of others, as when investors buy a stock simply because the company is recommended by a stockbroker or because everyone else is buying those shares. On the flip side, however, chapter 6 focuses on people's tendency toward overconfidence, which causes them to have more faith than they should in the reliability of their own judgment or experience. How can we reconcile these two concepts? We can't, really. The fact of the matter is that sometimes people make mistakes because they behave like sheep, and sometimes they err because they behave like mules. The critical task is to identify which tendency is harming us in what circumstance and then try to break the habit.

Which brings us to the last of our structural problems. Many readers would undoubtedly prefer that we could promise to "fix what ails them," with no qualifications or caveats. This, alas, we cannot do, but we hope that such an admission inspires trust and respect rather than dismissal. There is no single magic pill we can prescribe to eliminate all the mental money maladies from which you may suffer. What we can promise to do, however, is use our combined experience to offer suggestions for ways you can begin to eliminate troublesome behaviors. Some of these curatives are practical—involving, for instance, simple record keeping or investing in stock market index funds. Other solutions are more conceptual—instances in which we will try to change the way you frame a problem or situation that will make your choices clearer. In either case we'll offer these remedies at the end of each chapter, under the heading "How to Think and What to Do," and then summarize in the conclusion.

More important, though, we share a firmly held conviction that knowledge is the best medicine. If this book achieves its goal, it will provide numerous occasions when you'll smile (or grunt) in recognition at a money trap that has snared you in the past (it certainly has for each of us). That moment—that exposure of a particular mental blind spot—can do as much for your financial health as even the most helpful bit of advice that any financial adviser can give you.

Why Smart People Make Big Money Mistakes—and How to Correct Them

LESSONS FROM THE NEW SCIENCE OF BEHAVIORAL ECONOMICS

CHAPTER 1

NOT ALL DOLLARS ARE CREATED EQUAL

By the third day of their honeymoon in Las Vegas, the newlyweds had lost their $1,000 gambling allowance. That night in bed, the groom noticed a glowing object on the dresser. Upon closer inspection, he realized it was a $5 chip they had saved as a souvenir. Strangely, the number 17 was flashing on the chip's face. Taking this as an omen, he donned his green bathrobe and rushed down to the roulette tables, where he placed the $5 chip on the square marked 17. Sure enough, the ball hit 17 and the 35–1 bet paid $175. He let his winnings ride, and once again the little ball landed on 17, paying $6,125. And so it went, until the lucky groom was about to wager $7.5 million. Unfortunately the floor manager intervened, claiming that the casino didn't have the money to pay should 17 hit again. Undaunted, the groom taxied to a better-financed casino downtown. Once again he bet it all on 17—and once again it hit, paying more than $262 million. Ecstatic, he let his millions ride—only to lose it all when the ball fell on 18. Broke and dejected, the groom walked the several miles back to his hotel.

"Where were you?" asked his bride as he entered their room.

"Playing roulette."

"How did you do?"

"Not bad. I lost five dollars."

This story—told in some parts of Nevada as the gospel truth—has the distinction of being the only roulette joke we know that deals with a bedrock principle of behavioral economics. Indeed, depending on whether or not you agree with our groom's accounting of his evening's adventure, you might have an inkling as to why we considered a different title for this chapter, something like "Why Casinos Always Make Money." The conventional answer to that question—that casinos are consistently profitable because the odds for every game are stacked in favor of management—does not tell the whole story. Another reason casinos always make money is that too many people think like our newlywed: because he started his evening with just $5, he felt his loss was limited to that amount.

This view holds that his gambling spree winnings were somehow not real money—or not his money, in any event—and so his losses were not real losses. No matter that had the groom left the casino after his penultimate bet, he could have walked across the street and bought a brand-new Rolls-Royce for every behavioral economist in the country—and had enough left over to remain a multimillionaire. The happy salesman at the twenty-four-hour dealership—this is a Vegas story, after all—would never have thought to ask if the $262 million actually belonged to the groom. Of course it did. But the groom never really saw it that way. Like millions of amateur gamblers, he viewed his winnings as an entirely different kind of money and was therefore more willing to make extravagant bets with it. In casino-speak this is called playing with "house money." The tendency of most gamblers to fall prey to this illusion is why casinos would likely make out like bandits even if the odds were stacked less heavily in their favor.

The "Legend of the Man in the Green Bathrobe"—as the above tale is known—illustrates a concept that behavioral economists call "mental accounting." This idea, developed and championed by the University of Chicago's Richard Thaler, underlies one of the most common and costly money mistakes—the tendency to value some dollars less than others and thus to waste them. More formally, mental accounting refers to the inclination to categorize and treat money differently depending on where it comes from, where it is kept, or how it is spent. To understand how natural, and tricky, this habit can be, consider the following pair of scenarios. Here, as in similar mental exercises you'll find sprinkled throughout this book, try as best as you can to answer each question as realistically as possible. The more "honest" your responses, the more you'll learn about yourself.

Imagine that you've bought a ticket to the Super Bowl or a hit Broadway play. At the stadium or theater you realize you've lost your ticket, which cost $150. Do you spend another $150 to see the game or performance?

Now imagine the same scenario, but you're planning to buy the $150 ticket when you arrive. At the box office, you realize you've lost $150 *somewhere in the parking lot. Still, you have more than enough in your wallet to buy the ticket. Do you?*

If you're like most people, you probably answered "no" to the first question and "yes" to the second, even though both scenarios present the same dilemma: a loss of $150 and the subsequent prospect of spending another $150 to be entertained. The reason for this seeming inconsistency is that for most people the first scenario somehow translates into a total entertainment cost of $300—two actual tickets, each costing $150. This might be too much, even for a Super Bowl or hit play. Conversely, for most people the loss of $150 in cash and the $150 cost of the ticket are somehow separated—mentally—into two independent categories or accounts. They are unfortunate but unrelated. This type of thinking —treating two essentially equal $150 losses in very different ways because they occur in different manners—is a classic example of mental accounting.

The notion of mental accounts is anathema to traditional economics, which holds that wealth in general, and money in particular, should be "fungible." Fungibility, at its essence, means that $100 in roulette winnings, $100 in salary, and a $100 tax refund should have the same significance and value to you, since each Benjamin (as the kids like to say) could buy the same number of Happy Meals at McDonald's. Likewise, $100 kept under the mattress should invoke the same feelings or sense of wealth as $100 in a bank account or $100 in U.S. Treasury securities (ignoring the fact that money in the bank, or in T-bills, is safer than cash under the bed). If money and wealth are fungible, there should be no difference in the way we spend gambling winnings or salary. Every financial decision should result from a rational calculation of its effect on our overall wealth.

If only this were the case. In reality, as you probably have noticed, people are not computers. They lack the computational power and the strength of will necessary to manage all their finances on a consolidated balance sheet. It would be intellectually difficult, and emotionally taxing, to calculate the cost of every short-term transaction (buying a new compact disc, for instance, or going to a movie) against the size of every long-term goal or need (planning for retirement or saving for college). So to cope with this daunting organizational task, people separate their money into mental accounts, necessarily treating a dollar in one account differently from a dollar in another, since each account has a different significance. A vacation allowance, for instance, is presumably treated with less gravitas than the same amount of money socked away in an Individual Retirement Account.

But what's wrong with that? The average person, more self-aware, perhaps, than the average economist, knows that he or she is not as smart or as iron willed as economists maintain. And that's why people set up mental accounts in the first place. Thus, rather than being illogical or irrational, the ability to corral money into different mental accounts often has beneficial effects. Most important, perhaps, it allows you to save effectively for future goals. After all, "house money" for many Americans is not casino winnings, but the money they manage to squirrel away for a down payment on their dream home. Even profligate spenders manage to avoid tapping into these savings, often for no other reason than that they've placed it in a sacred mental vault. Certainly mental accounting is not always effective, given the problems human beings have with self-control. That's one of the reasons certain tax-deferred retirement accounts such as IRAs or Keogh plans penalize early withdrawals, and it is why they enjoy such popular support. And that is why, when attempting to balance and evaluate their investment portfolio, people often err by failing to knock down mental walls among accounts. As a result, their true portfolio mix

—the combination of stocks, bonds, real estate, mutual funds, and the like—is often not what they think, and their investment performance often suffers.

In any event, the sometimes useful habit of treating one dollar differently from another has a dark side as well, with consequences far more significant than simply increasing your willingness to make risky bets at roulette tables. By assigning relative values to different moneys that in absolute terms have the same buying power, you run the risk of being too quick to spend, too slow to save, or too conservative when you invest—all of which can cost you money. We'll get to all of that shortly, but the easiest-to-explain instance of mental accounting's harmful effects is the different value people place on earned income as opposed to gift income. That is, we'll spend $50 from Mom (or $50 we find in the street) with less thought than $50 we've earned on the job. Still, while such distinctions may be illogical from a strict economic point of view, they seem reasonable and harmless enough. After all, gift money—or casino winnings, for that matter—is generally "found" money. You didn't have it one second before you got it, so what's the harm in not having it again?

True enough. More troubling, though, and potentially more costly, is the tendency people have to "deposit" money in certain mental accounts when that money is actually part of another. Consider tax refunds, for example. Many people categorize such payments from the government as found money—and spend it accordingly—even though a refund is nothing more than a deferred payment of salary. Forced savings, if you will. If, on the other hand, those same people had taken that money out of their paycheck during the course of the previous year and deposited it into a bank account or money market mutual fund, they would most likely think long and hard before spending it on a new suit or Jacuzzi. However, because the "bank account" in which those funds have been sitting is run by Uncle Sam, taxpayers' mental accounting systems attach a different value to those dollars.

A DOLLAR HERE, A DOLLAR THERE—PRETTY SOON WE'RE TALKING ABOUT REAL MONEY

Another way mental accounting can cause trouble is the resultant tendency to treat dollars differently depending on the size of the particular mental account in which they are stashed, the size of the particular transaction in which they are spent, or simply the amount of money in question. Here's an illustration of what we mean:

Imagine that you go to a store to buy a lamp, which sells for $100. At the store you discover that the same lamp is on sale for $75 at a branch of the store five blocks away. Do you go to the other branch to get the lower price?

Now imagine that you go to the same store to buy a dining room set, which sells for $1,775. At the store you discover that you can buy the same table and chairs for $1,750 at a branch of the store five blocks away. Do you go to the other branch to get the lower price?

Once again, studies tell us that more people will go to the other branch to save on the lamp than would travel the same distance to save on the dining room set, even though both scenarios offer the same essential choice: Would you walk five blocks to save $25? You probably don't need to think long or hard to come up with instances in which this tendency can become quite costly (for you, that is—it's generally quite profitable for some salesperson). We certainly don't. As a struggling college student in the early 1980s, Gary had decided against replacing his car radio with a new cassette deck, for the simple reason that he couldn't justify the $300–$400 it would cost to buy the new piece of equipment. In his last year of college, though, Gary finally bought a new car (with the aid of a hefty auto loan). The cost: $12,000—plus another $550 for a cassette deck to replace the optional AM/FM radio. Three months earlier—before his car broke down—Gary had shopped for cassette decks and deemed $300 too extravagant. Yet a car salesman had little trouble convincing him to spend almost twice that amount for the same product, even though Gary's finances were presumably more precarious now that he had to make $180 monthly payments for the next four years.

The main culprit, of course, was mental accounting—$550 seemed to have less value next to $12,000. But also contributing to Gary's decision was the subconscious preference, shared by most people, to "integrate losses." Translation: When you incur a loss or expense, you prefer to hide it from yourself by burying it within a bigger loss or expense, so that the pain of spending $550 for a cassette deck was neutralized to a great extent by the larger pain of spending twelve grand.

Businesses, by the way, understand this tendency only too well. That's why consumer electronics stores sell extended warranties or service contracts with major purchases. Would anyone buy what is essentially an insurance policy for a CD player or TV at any other time? And it's why insurance agents sell exotic "riders" at the same time they're pushing broader policies. Would any rational person buy life insurance for, say, their young children if the policy was offered to them separately?

MYSTERY SOLVED

Mental accounting helps to explain one of the great puzzles of personal finance—why people who don't see themselves as reckless spenders can't seem to save enough. The devil, as they say, is in the details. Although many people are cost-conscious when making large financial decisions—such as buying a house, car, or appliance—mental accounting makes them relax their discipline when making small purchases. The cost of such purchases gets lost among larger expenses, such as the week's grocery bill, or charged against a lightly monitored "slush fund" account. The problem, of course, is that while you might purchase a car or refrigerator every few years, you buy groceries and clothes and movie refreshments every week or every day. Being cost-conscious when making little purchases is where you can often rack up big savings.

The principles of mental accounting are governed not only by the size of a purchase or investment, but also by the size of a payment received, be it a bonus, rebate, refund, or gift. Thus, a payment that might otherwise be placed in a discretionary mental account—a bonus at work, say, or a tax refund—will be deposited in a more serious, long-term account if it is big enough (and vice versa). That's curious, when you think about it. If you get a fairly small refund or bonus—let's say $250—chances are you're far more likely to buy a $250 pair of shoes with it than if you get a $2,500 bonus or refund, even though you can presumably afford it more in the second instance. Somehow, a bigger chunk of found money makes it more sacred and serious and harder to spend, actually lowering your "spending rate" (or what economists call the "marginal propensity to consume"). Understanding this concept can help you understand why it may be difficult for you to hold on to money and why a bonus or a gift may actually do you more harm than good. (Don't worry, though—our advice won't be to stop accepting gifts.) Your spending rate is simply the percentage of an incremental dollar that you spend rather than save. So if you receive a $100 tax refund and spend $80, your spending rate is .80 (or 80 percent). You might think, therefore, that the highest spending rate you can have is 1—that is, for every incremental dollar you receive, the most you could spend is a dollar. Alas, you'd be wrong. Let us explain.

About thirty years ago, an economist at the Bank of Israel named Michael Landsberger undertook a study of a group of Israelis who were receiving regular restitution payments from the West German government after World War II. Although these payments could without exaggeration be described as blood money—inasmuch as they were intended to make up for Nazi atrocities—they could also fairly accurately be described as found money. Because of this, and because the payments varied significantly in size from one individual or family to another, Landsberger was able to gauge the effect of the size of such windfalls on each recipient's spending rate. What he discovered was amazing. The group of recipients who received the larger payments (which were equal to about two-thirds of their annual income) had a spending rate of about 0.23. In other words, for every dollar they received, their marginal spending increased by 23 percent; the rest was saved. Conversely, the group that received the smallest windfall payments (equal to about 7 percent of annual income) had a spending rate of 2. That's correct: for every dollar of found money, they spent two. Or, more accurately, for every dollar of found money, they spent $1 of found money and another $1 from "savings" (what they actually saved or what they might have saved).

Obviously we can't explain this curious phenomenon with certainty. Perhaps restitution payments were made in proportion to a family's earlier earnings in Europe. If so, it may be that people who earned a lot before the war were also earning a lot in Israel and therefore had less pent-up "need" to spend their restitution checks. In Israel, like everywhere else, the wealthy save a higher proportion of their income than the poor. But this cannot explain why the spending rate of those receiving the smallest restitution payments was a whopping 200 percent. The poor are not helped by spending twice as much as they receive. A clearer understanding of this phenomenon may be obtained by considering the recent experience of a friend. This friend, let's call him Peter, works overseas for a small U.S. company. While on vacation in America, he stopped by corporate headquarters to say "hi" and, to his surprise, received a $400 bonus. Lucky, eh? Well, maybe not. By the end of his trip, Peter realized he had spent that $400 about five times over. It seems that every time he went into a store or restaurant, Peter and his wife used that $400 bonus to justify all manner of purchases. Not only was that bonus mentally accounted for as found money suitable for discretionary spending, it also sucked in $1,600 of the couple's money that had been accounted for otherwise.

FUNNY MONEY

Americanesia Expressaphobia, *n* 1. Financial affliction, first diagnosed in late twentieth century, in which the sufferer forgets the amount charged on a credit card but is terribly afraid that it's way too much. Closely related to **Visago,** *n,* in which a high level of debt prompts feeling of nausea and dizziness.

There's one more thing we ought to tell you about Peter's vacation saga, not least because we in no way want to discourage any bosses who might be reading this book from continuing to hand out bonuses, large or small. Much of Peter's shopping spree was abetted by credit cards, one of the scariest exhibits in the museum of mental accounting. In fact, credit cards and other types of revolving loans are almost by definition mental accounts, and dangerous ones at that. Credit card dollars are cheapened because there is seemingly no loss at the moment of purchase, at least on a visceral level. Think of it this way: If you have $100 cash in your pocket and you pay $50 for a toaster, you experience the purchase as cutting your pocket money in half. If you charge that toaster, though, you don't experience the same loss of buying power that emptying your wallet of $50 brings. In fact, the money we charge on plastic is devalued because it seems as if we're not actually spending anything when we use the cards. Sort of like Monopoly money. The irony, of course, is that the dollar we charge on plastic is actually more valuable, inasmuch as it costs an additional sixteen cents to spend it—16 percent or so being the typical interest rate for such borrowing.

Irony aside, we're not likely to surprise many readers by pointing out that credit cards play directly into the tendency to treat dollars differently. Because they seem to devalue dollars, credit cards cause you to spend money that you might not ordinarily spend. So common is credit card use and abuse today—at this writing the average U.S. consumer with revolving loans has more than $7,000 in credit card debt—that you've probably suffered a bout or two of Americanesia Expressaphobia yourself. No revelation there. But you may be surprised to learn that by using credit cards, you not only increase your chances of spending to begin with, you also increase the likelihood that you will pay *more* when you spend than you would if you were paying cash (or paying by check).

Want proof? Consider an experiment conducted several years ago by Drazen Prelec and Duncan Simester, marketing professors at the Massachusetts Institute of Technology in Cambridge, Massachusetts. The pair organized a real-life, sealed-bid auction for tickets to a Boston Celtics game (this was during the Larry Bird, Kevin McHale, Robert Parish era, so the tickets were especially valuable). Half the participants in the auction were informed that whoever won the bidding would have to pay for the tickets in cash (although they had a day to come up with the funds). The other half were told that the winning bidder would have to pay by credit card. Prelec and Simester then averaged the bids of those who thought they would have to pay in cash and those who thought they could pay with a credit card. Incredibly, the average credit card bid was roughly twice as large as the average cash bid. Simply because they were dealing with plastic—with money that was devalued in some way—the students became spendthrifts. Put another way, credit cards turn us into big spenders in more ways than one. We become poorer because we're more likely to spend, and more likely to spend poorly.

IT'S NOT GRANDMA'S MONEY

One final thought about mental accounting (at least for now). We've noted that the tendency to categorize, segregate, or label money differently can have the side effect of causing people to be more reckless with their money. Dollars assigned to some mental accounts are devalued, which leads us to spend more easily and more foolishly, particularly when dealing with small (though not inconsequential) amounts of money. But there's a flip side to this coin that can have the opposite effect—the tendency to mentally account for money as so sacred or special that we actually become too conservative with it.

The best way to demonstrate this phenomenon is with a story about a woman in her thirties named Sara. Sara is actually a fairly sophisticated investor, with a well-diversified portfolio of stocks and stock mutual funds. Good for her, considering that stocks have offered the best average annual return of all the major savings and investment categories over the past seventy years—about 11 percent a year on average, vs. 5 percent a year for bonds and 3 percent for cash in the bank. Several years ago, however, Sara inherited about $17,000 from her grandmother. Although she didn't need the money for any particular short-term or long-term goal, Sara parked her grandmother's inheritance in a bank account paying about 3 percent a year in interest. Her grandmother, whom Sara adored, had worked and saved all her life to scrape together the money that she eventually left to Sara and her four siblings. As a result, Sara was hesitant to put her grandmother's money at risk in the stock market, not least because Sara was raised by parents whose memory of the Great Depression and the stock market crash of 1929 made them and their daughter overly fearful about the risks of stocks. In any event, it didn't seem right to Sara, who would have been far more crushed if she lost "Grandma's money" than if she lost her own.

Her hesitation was costly. If Sara had simply invested that money as she does her other savings—in mutual funds that roughly approximated the overall performance of the stock market—she would now have more than $37,000. Instead, earning a meager 3 percent, she has just $18,600. Now it would be one thing if Sara had decided that she needed her grandmother's money for a specific short-term goal such as a down payment on a house, which would justify avoiding the stock market for fear of needing the money at just the time when stock prices were experiencing one of their inevitable dips. But Sara had no such constraint. Although other factors may cause people to be overly conservative with their investments, Sara's mistake was to mentally account for the $17,000 as "Grandma's money," or at least as money that was more sacred than her own savings and thus money that shouldn't be risked. In reality, of course, the money was hers, and the cost of her mental accounting was about $19,000.

Sara's mistake, we should add, is replicated by millions of Americans who choose the most conservative investment options in their 401(k), 403(b), and 457 plans at work because they mentally account for those funds as too sacred. This kind of thinking—"I have to be careful with my retirement money"—exposes you to a far more dangerous risk than the short-term ups and downs of the stock market: you run the risk that you won't have saved enough when your retirement finally rolls around.

HOW TO THINK AND WHAT TO DO

WARNING SIGNS

You may be prone to mental accounting if . . .

- you don't think you're a reckless spender, but you have trouble saving.
- you have savings in the bank *and* revolving balances on your credit cards.
- you're more likely to splurge with a tax refund than with savings.
- you seem to spend more when you use credit cards than when you use cash.
- most of your retirement savings are in fixed-income or other conservative investments.

How's this for practical advice about mental accounting: Stop it! If you charge too much on credit cards, cut 'em up. If you blow tax refunds at the track, cut it out. If only it were that easy. The difficulty with trying to remedy your tendency toward mental accounting is that you don't want to throw out the baby with the binge borrowing. For people who generally can't seem to control spending, mental accounts can often be the most effective way to ensure that the mortgage gets paid, the kids' colleges get funded, or there is enough money to live comfortably in retirement. And, of course, for every Sara who is too conservative with windfall money, there is someone else who would mentally account for an inheritance as gift money and blow it impulsively on a new stereo system. In fact, those two people may be one and the same—Sara may put inheritance money in one mental account, while stashing a tax refund or gambling winnings in another.

So in order to begin to eliminate the harmful elements of mental accounting, while preserving its benefits, you have to audit your own internal accounting system. We'll give you two ways to begin this process, one that's fun and one that's a bit more serious. First the fun stuff, in the form of another set of scenarios.

Imagine that you're at the racetrack for a day of gambling or at your favorite store shopping for a suit. Yesterday you won $1,000 from your state's instant lottery game. Will you bet more tonight than you would otherwise, or will you buy a more expensive suit?

Now imagine that you're once again at the racetrack for a day of gambling or at your favorite store shopping for a suit. Yesterday you realized that you had $1,000 in a savings account that you had forgotten about. Will you bet more tonight than you would otherwise, or will you buy a more expensive suit?

If you answered "yes" to the first question and "no" to the second —as most people would—you're prone to mental accounting, which means you're prone to wasting money because you wrongly put different values on the same dollars. No doubt skeptics will say that it is perfectly logical to be more reckless with lottery winnings than rediscovered savings, so what is Belsky and Gilovich's problem? Our problem is that while it may not make a difference if you blow a Lotto payoff, this habit can cost you money in ways you might not even think about. Our second test should help doubters see the light.

All you need to do is review your finances and answer two questions: 1) Do you have emergency or other nonretirement savings?; and 2) Do you carry balances on your credit cards from month to month?

If the answer is "yes" to both, you're a victim of mental accounting. Why? Because you've placed an inappropriately high value on your savings dollar and too low a value on your borrowed dollars. As a result, you're likely earning 5 percent a year on your emergency savings, while paying 16 percent a year in credit card interest. For every $1,000 on your credit card, that's a yearly loss of roughly $110. If you do nothing else after reading this but pay off $1,000 in credit card balances with short-term savings, then you've earned the price of this book about five times over. And for those people who say that emergency money should be left just for emergencies, our response is that if you pay off your credit card balances with short-term savings, you could always fill up those same credit cards in the event that you or your spouse is laid off or laid up. Believe us when we tell you that your credit card company won't cut or eliminate your access to their high-rate loans if you pay off your balances. More than likely they'll raise your credit limit, so that you'll be that much more prepared for "emergencies." And all the while you'll be saving the difference between the money you would have been paying in interest and the money you would have earned from a money market account.

Imagine a world without plastic. No, we're not suggesting you deep-six your Visa or Sears card. We're just recommending that you start asking yourself how much you would pay for a prospective purchase if you were paying cash out of your pocket. You might answer that you would pay a lot less than you're willing to charge or even that you wouldn't make the purchase at all.

See the trees for the forest. That's another way of saying that when you make a big purchase or investment—such as a car or a house —break every deal into its component part. Would you, say, pay $3,000 to put a skylight into the den of your current house? If not, then don't tack on that extra when contracting for a new home— $3,000 may not seem like a lot when you're buying a $150,000 home, but it buys just as much as $3,000 in your checking account (more, actually, when you count the interest you'll pay over the course of your loan).

Hurry up and wait. To the extent that you fall prey to the tendency to view windfall money—tax refunds, gifts, inheritances, or bonuses—as found money that can be spent relatively carelessly, our advice is to train yourself to wait a while before making any spending decisions. In other words, tell yourself that you can do whatever you want with that cash, but in three or six months. In the meantime, park it in a bank or money market account. Make that the rule. At the least you'll have a few extra dollars for your trouble. More than likely, by the time your deadline rolls around you'll view this money as savings—hard earned and not to be wasted.

Imagine that all income is earned income. This idea for dealing with money that you didn't earn—or even money for which you did work—may be the best way to train yourself to view all your money equally. Basically, the trick is to ask yourself how long it would take you to earn that amount of money after taxes. Quite often the answer will clear up your accounting problems faster than you can say "marginal tax rate."

Use mental accounting to your advantage. This kernel of counsel is essentially an endorsement for payroll deduction plans. Folks who have difficulty holding on to small amounts of money often have difficulty saving, for the obvious reason that small amounts are what are left in our paychecks after we pay the bills. That's where labeling tricks can help. By funneling money into a mutual fund or savings account directly from your paycheck, $50 that you might have accounted for as bowling money and spent easily is mentally (and physically) accounted for as savings—and thus less likely to be wasted and more likely to be around when you need it.

There is another reason that payroll deduction plans are a good idea, one that involves an important psychological principle we discuss in the next chapter. Psychologically it's much easier to part with your money—to set it aside—this way than by writing a check to your savings account. Let us explain why.

CHAPTER 2

WHEN SIX OF ONE ISN'T HALF A DOZEN OF THE OTHER

Imagine that you're a commander in the army, threatened by a superior enemy force. Your staff says your soldiers will be caught in an ambush in which six hundred of them will die unless you lead them to safety by one of two available routes. If you take route A, two hundred soldiers will be saved. If you take route B, there's a one-third chance that six hundred soldiers will be saved and a two-thirds chance that none will be saved. Which route should you take?

If you ever have occasion to read the thousands of scholarly books and articles written about behavioral economics—and, further straining belief, if you conscientiously read the bibliography at the end of each one—you'll notice that one article is referenced in these works more than any other, by far. Written by Daniel Kahneman and Amos Tversky and published in the March 1979 issue of the wonderfully named journal *Econometrica,* the article is titled "Prospect Theory: An Analysis of Decision under Risk." If Richard Thaler's concept of mental accounting is one of two pillars upon which the whole of behavioral economics rests, then prospect theory is the other. Like mental accounting, prospect theory deals with the way we frame decisions, the different ways we label—or code—outcomes, and how they affect our attitude toward risk. As we shall see, the same outcome can often be described either in the vocabulary of gains or in the vocabulary of losses, and such unconscious and inconsistent coding has far-reaching effects. Indeed, we might just as easily have constructed this book as one long essay explaining prospect theory and all of the ideas that flow from it—that's how influential and seminal the ideas discussed in Kahneman and Tversky's paper are.

Instead we've divided the ramifications of prospect theory—and the asymmetry in the way people treat losses and gains—into a pair of basic concepts. The first, which we'll discuss in this chapter, is the way that our feelings about loss—called "loss aversion" in psychoeconomic lingo—and our inability to forget money that's already been spent—termed the "sunk cost fallacy"—make us too ready to throw good money after bad. Later, in the next chapter, we'll explore the second concept: how a preference for keeping things the way they are—the "status quo bias"—combines with a tendency to fall in love with what we own—the "endowment effect"—to make us resist change. A deeper understanding of these two concepts should lead you to better investment and spending decisions.

RISKY BUSINESS

Imagine that you're once again a commander in the army, threatened by a superior enemy force. Once again, your staff tells you that if you take route A, four hundred soldiers will die. If you take route B, there's a one-third chance that no soldiers will die and a two-thirds chance that six hundred soldiers will perish. Which route should you choose?

Take another look at the scenario laid out at the beginning of this chapter—which, like the one you just read, was constructed by writer Kevin McKean for a 1985 article on Kahneman and Tversky in *Discover* magazine. The scenarios, you may have noticed, are subtly—but significantly—different from each other. Indeed, research conducted by the two Israeli psychologists suggests that more than likely you chose the first route in the first scenario (where two hundred soldiers would be saved) but the second route in the second (where there is a one-third chance that no one will be killed). What's curious about this is that the final outcome in both versions, for both the first and second options, *is exactly the same.* With route A—the sure saving of two hundred lives in the first version or the sure loss of four hundred in the second—you end up with two hundred lives saved and four hundred casualties in either case. With route B you would have a one-third chance of saving six hundred soldiers and a two-thirds chance of losing them all.

But by choosing route A in the first case and route B in the second, people demonstrate how different their decisions can be depending on how they frame the problem. When the scenario is framed as a matter of how many lives might be saved, the tendency is to be cautious, to save as many as possible. But when the scenario is framed in terms of lives lost, the tendency is to be more adventurous, to gamble in the hopes of saving everybody rather than ensuring the death of four hundred soldiers.

In financial matters this phenomenon results in a willingness to take more risk if it means avoiding a sure loss and to be more conservative when given the opportunity to lock in a sure gain. Not sure what we mean? Take a look at the next two scenarios and the concept should become a little clearer.

Imagine that you have just been given $1,000 and have been asked to choose between two options. With option A you are guaranteed to win an additional $500. With option B you are given the chance to flip a coin. If it's heads, you receive another $1,000; tails, you get nothing more. Which option would you choose?

Now imagine that you have just been given $2,000 and are required to choose between two options. With option A you are guaranteed to lose $500. With option B you are given the chance to flip a coin. If it's heads, you lose $1,000; tails, you lose nothing. Now which option would you choose?

Once again, research suggests that more than likely you chose option A in the first scenario (the sure gain of $500) but option B in the second (an even chance to lose $1,000 or nothing at all). And, again, the final outcome in both versions, for both options A and B, is the same. With option A—the sure gain in the first version or the sure loss in the second—you end up with $1,500 in either scenario. With option B you have an even chance of winding up with $1,000 or $2,000 in both the first and second scenario. But by choosing option A in the first case and option B in the second, you once again show that you're willing to take more risk if it means avoiding losses and to be more conservative when given the opportunity to lock in sure profits. This outlook, by the way, is one of the reasons gamblers often increase their bets when chance is not going their way; they're willing to take a bigger risk to avoid finishing in the red.

The reason for this difference in outlook can be found in a psychological principle known as "Weber's law," named after the nineteenth-century German physiologist Ernst Weber. Although most people are unlikely to know it by name, they nonetheless know the phenomenon itself—that, loosely speaking, the impact of a change in the intensity of a stimulus is proportional to the absolute level of the original stimulus. In real life it means you are likely to notice if someone goes to a tanning booth in January, but not in July. In financial terms the difference between earning $10 or $20 for a job well done has a bigger effect on how happy you are than a difference between earning $110 or $120.

Weber's law implies that people will be cautious when dealing with potential gains. The difference between nothing and $500 is greater psychologically than the difference between $500 and $1,000, so most people want to lock in the sure $500. The same law, however, implies a greater tolerance for risk when dealing with potential losses. Again, the difference between losing $500 and losing nothing is greater psychologically than that between losing $500 and losing $1,000. Why not expose yourself, then, to the risk of losing that last (relatively unimportant) $500 in exchange for the possibility of sustaining no loss at all?

Prospect theory, boiled down to its essence, is an attempt to incorporate Weber's law and a great many other psychological principles to explain why people choose the way they do. Our mission, boiled down to *its* essence, is to explain how the different ways people code gains and losses can lead to poor investing and spending decisions. Traditional economics suggests that your inclination to choose option A should be no stronger in either of the two situations just described because your final asset position in either case is the same: you wind up with $1,500 more than you had before behavioral economists started handing out free money. The only choice that matters, then, should be whether you prefer the certain $1,500 or the gamble that offers you an even chance of having either one grand or two. That's what traditional economic theory suggests, anyway.

Prospect theory, on the other hand, offers an alternative way to look at things. It says that people generally do not assign values to options based on the options' expected effect on their overall level of wealth: the typical head of an American family, with a net worth of $200,000 or so, doesn't see a $500 loss or gain as one-fourth of 1 percent of her overall financial position. She sees it as $500 that she did or didn't have five minutes before she lost or gained it. Indeed, prospect theory says that we assign values to the gains or losses themselves—based on their own merits, if you will, as gains or losses. It is the actual gaining or losing—and our feelings about it—that matter more to us, rather than how those gains or losses leave us in terms of our overall financial position.

People's reactions to gains and losses highlight a very important feature of human judgment, namely, that judgments are constructed "on the spot" in response to specific tasks and are therefore very sensitive to how the problems arise or the way in which they are framed. For example, you might think that if someone prefers a cellular phone to extra coverage on an automobile insurance policy, then he should be willing to pay more for the cell phone. Not so, or at least not always so. Choosing and pricing call upon different psychological processes, so there are times when a person will choose the cell phone but pay more for the insurance policy. Likewise, you might think that the similarity between, say, *a mother and her daughter* would be the same as that between the very same *daughter and her mother.* Not so. People assess similarity differently depending on the direction from which they start, which is why people typically report that North Korea seems more similar to China than China seems to North Korea. Finally, you might think that if one pair of items is more similar to one another than another pair—oranges and apples vs. shovels and spoons—then they also have to be less *dissimilar.* Again, not so. Assessments of similarity call upon different psychological processes than assessments of dissimilarity, so it is possible for one pair to be both more similar and more dissimilar than another pair. Slightly different twists on the same questions can enlist different modes of thought and therefore lead to very distinct responses.

IT DEPENDS ON HOW YOU LOOK AT IT

New York Yankees legend Yogi Berra reportedly was once asked into how many slices he wanted his pizza cut. Berra's alleged reply: "You better make it four; I'm not hungry enough to eat eight."

The importance of how a decision is approached—or how it is framed—is nicely illustrated by an experiment conducted by Princeton University psychologist Eldar Shafir. Shafir presented one group of students with the following question:

Imagine that you are planning a week's vacation in a warm spot over spring break. You currently have two options that are reasonably priced. The travel brochure gives only a limited amount of information about the two options. Given the information available, which vacation spot would you prefer?

Spot A: *Average weather*	***Spot B:*** *Lots of sunshine*
Average beaches	*Gorgeous beaches/coral reef*
Medium-quality hotel	*Ultramodern hotel*
Medium-temperature water	*Very cold water*
Average nightlife	*Very strong winds*
	No nightlife

The other half of the students Shafir interviewed were offered the same selection of vacation spots but with a slightly different frame of reference for their decision, marked by us in bold.

Imagine that you are planning a week's vacation in a warm spot over spring break. You currently have two options that are reasonably priced, ***but you can no longer retain both reservations.*** *The travel brochure gives only a limited amount of information about the two options. Given the information available, which* ***reservation do you decide to cancel?***

As you can see, both sets of students were asked to make the same decision—where to spend their vacation. However, one group viewed the problem as one of selection (which spot was preferable), and the other as one of rejection (which one to cancel). That difference was significant. Of the students who were asked which spot they *preferred,* 67 percent opted for spot B. Conversely, 48 percent chose to cancel their reservations for spot B. Spot B, in other words, somehow has more appeal when choosing (67 percent chose it) than when rejecting (only 52 percent kept it).

What happens, as Shafir explained, is that when people view a decision as one of preference, they tend to focus on the positive qualities of the options they are considering. So although spot B had more negatives than spot A, it also had more obvious positive attributes. In contrast, when asked to cancel a reservation, people tend to focus more on the negative qualities of each option. So students who might have otherwise preferred spot B because of its more compelling weather, scenery, and accommodations were thinking more about what they didn't like. As a result, more students chose to cancel their reservation to spot B.

Getting back to people's emotions about gaining versus losing money, what's important to understand is that, according to prospect theory, people feel more strongly about the pain that comes with loss than they do about the pleasure that comes with an equal gain. About twice as strongly, according to Kahneman and Tversky, meaning that people feel the misery of losing $100 (or $1,000 or $1 million) about twice as keenly as they feel the pleasure of gaining a like amount. That's why you are likely to choose the sure gain of $500 in the first scenario but reject the sure loss of $500 in the second, even though both would leave you with $1,500. The idea of losing $500—for certain—is so painful that you're willing to take a risk of winding up with a mere $1,000 simply to avoid that discomfort. Similarly, in a sort of mirror effect, the idea of letting that $500 gain in the first scenario slip away, for the chance of maybe winding up with a $1,000 gain, is discomfiting enough to cause you to opt for the sure thing.

KNOW WHEN TO HOLD 'EM; KNOW WHEN TO FOLD 'EM

At this point, some readers may object to the implication that loss aversion is a bad thing. They might justifiably point out that the tendency to weight losses more heavily than gains is in many respects a net positive. After all, beings who care too much about possible gains and too little about potential losses run too great a risk of experiencing the kinds of losses that threaten their survival. Better to care more about falling too far than climbing so high.

True enough. Loss aversion can be helpful and conservative (in the nonpolitical sense). But an oversensitivity to loss can also have negative consequences. One of the most obvious and important areas in which loss aversion skews judgment is in investing. In the short term, being especially sensitive to losses contributes to the panic selling that accompanies stock market crashes (we'll discuss other causes later). The Dow Jones Industrial Average tumbles (along with stock prices and mutual fund shares in general), and the pain of these losses makes many investors overreact: the injured want to stop the bleeding. The problem, of course, is that pulling your money out of the stock market on such a willy-nilly basis leaves you vulnerable to a different sort of pain—the pangs you'll feel when stock prices rise while you're licking your wounds.

And don't be fooled into thinking you can make amends for your low pain threshold by jumping back into the market once you regain your senses. Although stocks seem to rise steadily over time, they actually do so in major fits and starts—a few big gains on a small number of days sprinkled throughout the year. Indeed, the stock market is much like that common description of war: long periods of boredom interrupted by episodes of pure terror. By pulling your money out in reaction to short-term drops, you run the risk of missing those productive days. And it's a serious risk. According to a study conducted in 1994 by University of Michigan finance professor H. Nejat Seyhun, if you had missed the forty best-performing days of the stock market from 1963 to 1993, your average annual return would have dropped from almost 12 percent, assuming you had stayed fully invested, to slightly more than 7 percent. And there were 7,802 trading days over that period, so we're talking about missing only 0.012 percent of the action. On a

$10,000 investment, those different rates of return translate into the difference between having $233,000 after three decades or having about $80,000.

In any event, being overly sensitive to the pain of losing money can sometimes make us too quick to abandon investments. What's tricky about this concept, though, is that loss aversion can often lead us in the opposite direction—to *hold on* to losing investments for longer than we should. Ask yourself if you've ever sold a stock not because you thought it was finished rising, but because you wanted to "lock in profits." And ask yourself how many times you've held on to a losing stock or mutual fund (or home or piece of art) because you were sure it would "come back."

HOME ECONOMICS

Loss aversion doesn't affect only securities investments. A woman Gary knows bought a condo in Boston in the late 1980s for $110,000, just before the real estate market in the Northeast collapsed. A year later, when her job forced her to move to another city, the highest offer she received for her place was $100,000. She passed, less because she thought the real estate market would improve than because she was unable to face the prospect of taking a $10,000 loss. Instead she leased an apartment in Los Angeles while simultaneously renting out her Boston home. Eventually, though, she was forced to sell her condo when she decided to buy a home in Los Angeles. Her selling price: $92,000. No need to wonder why an overdeveloped fear of losses can lead anybody to make financial decisions that are not in their best interest.

Even if these questions don't ring true for you, it's a fact that individual investors tend to sell winning investments too quickly and keep losing ones too long. It was verified in 1997 by Terrance Odean, a graduate student at the Haas School of Business at the University of California at Berkeley. Odean, who's now on the faculty at the University of California–Davis, analyzed the trading records of ten thousand accounts at a large national discount brokerage firm over a seven-year period beginning in 1987 and ending in 1993. Among other findings, his gargantuan research effort highlighted a pair of remarkable facts. First, investors *were* in fact more likely to sell stocks that had risen in price rather than those that had fallen.

Think about this in nautical terms: Your investments are the flotilla that you hope will carry you to the shores of a secure retirement over the choppy seas of life. But rather than sticking with boats that have proven their seaworthiness, you routinely abandon ship in favor of dinghies that have already sprung some leaks. Now this may strike you as perfectly logical, particularly if you're a person who sells winners more often than losers. The argument for this sort of reasoning would be that the winners have already had their run, while the losing stocks have yet to make their move. It's a version of the regression theory discussed in the introduction to this book: The seaworthy boats (which had their tailwind of good fortune) are due to spring some leaks, while it's about time the leaky boats become more secure. So, better to sell the good boats now before they sink.

Obviously no sailor in his right mind would behave in this fashion, yet many investors do so routinely.

And Odean's data show the folly of most investors' behavior. According to his research, the stocks that investors *sold* outperformed the stocks that they held on to by 3.4 percentage points over the ensuing twelve months. In other words, investors sold the stocks they should have kept and kept the stocks they should have sold. And remember, this isn't an occasional result; it's a persistent pattern among thousands of investors studied by Odean. What makes Odean's research even more extraordinary is that when you sell an investment at a loss, the Internal Revenue Service allows you to reduce your taxable income by the amount of the loss, up to $3,000 (presuming you have no capital gains in the same year against which you can apply your losses). So Uncle Sam stands ready, whenever you're willing to take a loss, to subsidize it for you. Yet people still refuse to "book the loss."

Now, we could spend a great deal of time considering all the reasons that might cause investors to make this expensive mistake over and over again. Odean, in fact, raised many: "Alternative explanations have been proposed for why investors might realize [gains on] their profitable investments while retaining their losing investments. Investors may rationally, or irrationally, believe that their current losers will outperform their current winners. They may sell winners to rebalance their portfolios. Or they may refrain from selling losers due to the higher transaction costs of trading at lower prices. I find, however, that when the data are controlled for rebalancing and share price, the disposition effect is still observed."

The "disposition effect" that Odean refers to is the name that Hersh M. Shefrin and Meir Statman, then of Santa Clara University, gave in 1985 to the tendency to hold losers too long and sell winners too soon. It is, in effect, an extension of prospect theory and loss aversion. Most people are much more willing to lock in the sure gain that comes with selling a winning stock or fund than they are willing to lock in the sure loss of selling a losing investment, even though it generally makes more sense to sell the losers and keep the winners. The prospect of selling that losing investment (and the pain associated with making the loss final) makes them more willing to dig in their heels and take risks—the risk, of course, being that if they hold on to the losers, the investment will continue to drop in price. After all, until you actually sell a losing investment the drop in price is only a "paper loss"—it's not official. Once you sell it, though, it's real. This, of course, is creative mental accounting at its worst: the unrealized losses are segregated or compartmentalized in a separate account precisely *because* they're unrealized. Thus you can ignore them (or treat them as a potential future gain) and they don't disprove your investing "prowess."

Losing investments, then, represent a variation of the choice presented in the second scenario earlier in this chapter: option A, sell and guarantee a loss; or option B, hold on and risk losing more for the opportunity to get your money back. Winning investments, on the other hand, represent a variation of the choice presented in the first scenario: option A, sell and guarantee a gain; or option B, hold on and risk losing your profit for the opportunity to earn more. Loss aversion tells us it is less painful—and more common—to sell winners and keep losers. Odean's research says it's a lot smarter to do the opposite.

One final thought about loss aversion: Kahneman and Tversky noted that being overly sensitive to loss leads people to opt for a certain gain over one that offers a high possibility of a larger gain. In real life that usually translates into a preference for fixed-income investments over stocks. A guaranteed 6 percent or 7 percent annual return from Uncle Sam may seem a lot more appealing than the "chance" to earn 11 percent or more a year in stocks. But as we'll see later on, the dangers of the stock market may not be as important as the ravages of inflation. So to the extent that you opt for "safe" investments—such as bonds, annuities, and other fixed-income or life insurance products—over riskier but generally higher-paying ones, your loss aversion may be costing you a lot of money.

GOOD MONEY AFTER BAD

Imagine that you've been given courtside tickets to a Chicago Bulls basketball game or a performance of a classic ballet. You're dying to go because you want to see Michael Jordan or Mikhail Baryshnikov before he retires. Before you leave your house, you learn that Jordan is injured and won't play, or that Baryshnikov won't perform. Plus, a sudden snowstorm makes the trip to the game or ballet unpleasant and somewhat dangerous. Do you go?

Now imagine the same game or ballet, except in this instance you paid a small fortune for the ticket yourself and there's no chance of selling it to someone else. Do you go?

A particular form of loss aversion to which we are all prone is what Richard Thaler described in 1980 as the "sunk cost fallacy." This psychological trap is the primary reason most people would choose to risk traveling in a dangerous snowstorm if they had paid for a ticket to an important game or ballet, while passing on the trip if they had been given the ticket for free. The distinction makes no sense, of course: the money for the ticket is spent—or sunk—in either case; you won't get it back whether you go to the event or watch it on television. As a matter of fact, going to the game or ballet means incurring an extra cost: the chance that you might die or be seriously injured. Therefore the danger posed by the snowstorm should carry equal significance for people who receive the ticket for free or pay for it. That it doesn't—that there is more significance because we have sunk money into the deal, regardless of whether or not that money can be retrieved—is an example of the sunk cost fallacy. And this isn't just hypothetical theorizing.

For a 1985 research paper entitled "The Psychology of Sunk Cost," published in the journal *Organizational Behavior and Human Decision Processes,* Hal R. Arkes and Catherine Blumer of Ohio University conducted an interesting real-life experiment. They randomly distributed discounts to buyers of subscriptions to Ohio University Theater's 1982–1983 season. One group of buyers paid the normal ticket price of $15; a second group received a $2 discount per ticket; and a third sampling of lucky theater lovers received $7 off each ticket. Members of the last two groups were told that the discount was being given as part of a promotion by the theater department. The result? The people who paid more for their tickets ended up attending the performances more often than those who had received discounts.

Logically there should not have been any difference in attendance. Not only did all the groups presumably have similar inclinations to attend when they bought their tickets, they all were prepared to pay the same ticket price and they all had the same tickets in hand as the season progressed. Although this phenomenon tended to lessen—predictably—as the theater season progressed (farther away from the original date of purchase), the conclusion of the experiment is unavoidable: The more people spent on their tickets, the greater their sunk costs, and the more seriously they took attendance at the plays.

Arkes and Blumer labored mightily to explain why sunk costs have such a powerful effect on people, beyond the obvious, though irrational, notion of loss aversion: If people didn't go to a performance, they likely equated the unused ticket with a loss. Therefore the higher their ticket price, the greater the loss to be averted and the greater the likelihood that they would expend effort to see the performances. No matter that the money was already spent whether they went to the play or stayed home and vegged on the couch. One of the more interesting suggestions that the researchers made

—the one that we're inclined to agree with—is that people fall prey to the sunk cost fallacy because they don't want to appear wasteful. Not necessarily to other people, mind you; most people act as their own judge and jury when it comes to their own finances. In any case, Arkes and Blumer buttress their point with the results from the following scenario, which was posed to eighty-nine survey participants:

On your way home you buy a TV dinner on sale for $3 at the local grocery store. A few hours later you decide it is time for dinner, so you get ready to put the TV dinner in the oven. Then you get an idea. You call up your friend to ask if he would like to come over for a quick TV dinner and then watch a good movie on TV. Your friend says sure. You go out to buy a second TV dinner. However, all the on-sale TV dinners are gone. You therefore have to spend $5 (the regular price) for the TV dinner identical to the one you just bought for $3. You go home and put both dinners in the oven. When the two dinners are fully cooked, you get a phone call. Your friend is ill and cannot come. You are not hungry enough to eat both dinners. You cannot freeze one. You must eat one and discard the other. Which one do you eat?

Not surprisingly, the majority of participants in the survey (sixty-six) expressed no preference, since the costs and benefits of choosing either dinner are the same: you've spent eight bucks, and no matter which dinner you eat, one of the meals will go to waste. Amazingly, though, twenty-one people said they would eat the $5 dinner, a choice that Arkes and Blumer suggest can only be the result of those folks having the impression that throwing away a $5 meal would be more wasteful than throwing away a $3 meal. (As for the two people who said they would eat the $3 meal, your guess is as good as Arkes and Blumer's.)

Whatever the causes of the sunk cost fallacy, the importance of ignoring money already spent and focusing on future costs and benefits should be obvious. If it's not, ask yourself how many times you've opted to repair a car or furnace, or to spend money on some other endeavor, based largely or entirely on the fact that you've already invested so much. Here's a personal example from our files: When Gary was in college and learning to play hockey, he bought a pair of goaltender leg pads for $350. Truth be told, Gary discovered quickly that he had little potential as a goalie. But when the time came to buy more equipment, he opted to purchase skates, sticks, gloves, and shoulder pads that were designed especially for goaltenders. Why? Because he had already spent such a large amount on the leg pads, and because facing up to his weakness in goal was difficult. You won't be surprised to hear the conclusion to this tale: Eventually Gary figured out that his future lay elsewhere on the ice. The used leg pads, along with $650 spent on the other equipment, were eventually resold for a grand total of $400. His initial sunk cost: $350; his final loss: $600.

It turns out that the sunk cost fallacy affects your pocketbook in more ways than you might first imagine, including your taxes. Arkes and Blumer observed that government spending decisions are often based on how much has already been spent. They noted that during late 1981 funding for the very expensive Tennessee-Tombigbee Waterway Project was scheduled for congressional review. In defending the project, Tennessee senator James Sasser remarked: "Completing Tennessee-Tombigbee is not a waste of taxpayer dollars. Terminating the project at this late stage of development would, however, represent a serious waste of funds already invested." In other words, good project or not, we have to finish it because we've already spent so much money on it. No matter that the money is already gone. Arkes and Blumer wisely point out that canny folks who are aware of the sunk cost fallacy can use it to their advantage. They cite a 1981 article in *Mother Jones,* in which a nuclear power industry executive is quoted as saying: "When it comes down to it, no one with any sense would abort a $2.5 billion construction project. And, by extension, no administration would abort a $200 billion national investment in nuclear energy. So the trick for the industry is to get more new plants under construction without the (antinuclear) movement knowing about it. By the time they get around to demonstrating and challenging the license, we'll have a million tons of steel and concrete in the ground, and no one in their right minds will stop us." Thus a common gambit in the world of government is to get as much money as possible spent on a favorite project so that it is protected by the sunk cost fallacy by the time more sober minds and more rational analysis point out its flaws.

HOW TO THINK AND WHAT TO DO

WARNING SIGNS

You might be a victim of loss aversion or the sunk cost fallacy if . . .

- you make important spending decisions based on how much you've already spent.
- you generally prefer bonds over stocks.
- you tend to sell winning investments more readily than losing ones.
- you're seriously tempted to take money out of the stock market when prices fall.

Throughout this book we'll gradually build an argument that many individuals should consider an automatic approach to investing by relying primarily on mutual funds—specifically index mutual funds, which attempt to do no more than mimic the performance of the stock and bond markets in general. That said, many of you might not want to scale back your active involvement in your portfolio. After all, it's fun. Moreover, loss aversion and the sunk cost fallacy have pronounced effects beyond the decision to buy or sell a stock or bond. So here are several suggestions that should help you make wiser decisions no matter what the issue.

Test your threshold for loss. Broadly, the best advice we can give you regarding loss aversion is to assume that you are probably more sensitive to losing money—in one way or another—than you think. If you operate under that assumption, you're more likely to avoid making decisions that will get you into trouble when you realize, retrospectively, that you exposed yourself to more risk than you were willing or able to deal with properly. Still, most people are not keen to admit that they're prone to any of the psychological traps we discuss in this book, particularly those folks who pride themselves on their investing acumen. And, in fact, you may be the smartest, most rational investor in the world. Or maybe you just think you are.

That's why it's important to assess your level of loss aversion, which is another way of saying that you should evaluate your tolerance for risk. As we mentioned earlier, loss aversion can have two very different effects, so you need to ask two very different types of questions. The first aims to let you know if you're likely to be quick to abandon ship—if your aversion to loss is so great that you'll panic at the first sign of real trouble. That's an especially relevant question to ask today, since this book is being written during an unusually long period of rising stock prices. So be honest and ask yourself: "If the stock market drops 25 percent tomorrow, would I be tempted to pull all or some of my money out?" If the answer is "yes," you're probably unprepared for the ups and downs of the stock market.

The second type of question should help you see if your brand of loss aversion is likely to lead you to dig in your heels on bad investments. Consider the following query and, again, answer as realistically as you can: Say you have $10,000 of Microsoft stock that you bought for $5,000, and $10,000 of IBM stock that you bought for $20,000. Your child's first-semester tuition bill of $10,000 is due. Which stock would you sell? If your answer is the Microsoft, you're mortal like the rest of us. And your aversion to loss is likely to leave you poorer than you need to be. (The best strategy, perhaps, might be to sell $5,000 worth of each company's stock, thus avoiding the need to pay any taxes!)

Diversify. The best way to avoid the pain of losing money, of course, is to avoid losing money. We haven't figured that one out yet, but there are ways to minimize investment losses. One of the best is *diversification:* doling out your investment portfolio among stocks (or stock mutual funds), bonds (or bond mutual funds), money market funds, even real estate (if you don't own a house, then ideally through real estate investment trusts). We'll omit portfolio allocation theory and other types of investment advice for now, but the behavioral-economic idea behind diversification is that a loss in one portion of your nest egg—say, your stock investments—will likely be offset by gains in another—say, bonds or real estate. So you'll be less likely to react emotionally and do something drastic if at the same time that you take a hit you are also experiencing gains in another part of your portfolio.

There's another reason we strongly advocate diversification. You needn't be a psychic to deduce that we believe stocks are the best way for most Americans to build wealth. This view is based on the historical performance of stocks over the past seven decades or so, which we discuss more fully elsewhere in these pages. That said, we would be negligent if we didn't throw up a warning flare. As mentioned, we're writing this during one of the greatest bull markets in history. It is, quite frankly, an environment in which share prices seem headed for a fall, if for no other reason than history *also* teaches us that stocks tend to underperform for a while after they outperform. Of course, we can't know for certain when or if that drop will happen. No one can, which is basically the point of this brief intermission. What we want to do is explain why you can't count on stocks to perform as well in the future as they have in the past, and then explain why you nonetheless have little choice but to rely on stocks as the driving engine of your investment portfolio. Here we go:

The problem with the now commonly held notion that the stock market is the best way for individuals to get rich is that this view is based on the past. But if you think about this, it is probably naive to look at seventy years of recent financial history and use it as the definitive model for the future. What if the past seven decades have been no more than an aberration, a blip in the millennia-long history of wealth accumulation on this planet? It's a bit like evaluating a baseball player's potential based on one week's play. Three home runs in one game doesn't mean that player will be as prolific a batsman as Babe Ruth. Likewise, just because stocks have been a great investment for seventy years doesn't mean they will be a great investment in the future. They could be, most certainly, but there's no way to know. Past performance really is no guarantee of future results, or even a very reliable gauge.

The point we're trying to hammer home is that there are no guarantees that any asset will thrive in the future as it has in the past. That leaves you with two options: 1) keep your money under a mattress and hope that you save enough during your working years to last in retirement; or 2) take some risk and invest your money in assets that have a reasonable chance to increase in value over time. For most people, 1) isn't really an option, if only because most people can't save enough after living expenses to support themselves in retirement, especially during eras (like the current one) when inflation exists and erodes the buying power of money.

That leaves 2), and since you have to do *something* with your money, the issue becomes a matter of picking the assets with which to cast your lot. And that brings us full circle. Although there are many sound reasons to invest in stocks—the most important being that stocks increase in value faster than inflation decreases the buying power of money—the philosophical rationale for making stocks the largest slice of your investment pie boils down to this: If you think about it, the best way to guarantee that you'll *have* money in the future is to *make* money in the future. That is, forget about trying to predict which assets will increase in value and focus instead on owning a business that profitably sells products or services for substantially less than it costs to provide them. Of course, most people don't have the inclination or the money or the skill to start their own business, so the next best way to share in the profits is through the stock market. Stocks, remember, represent ownership interest in businesses. When you invest in the stock market you become a partial owner of concerns that (hopefully) will make money regardless of economic conditions in the future. You're betting on the collective growth potential of (primarily) U.S. businesses. Logic dictates that the owners of such firms will eventually be rewarded, either because share prices will rise or because the firms' profits will be distributed as dividends.

To be sure, it is unlikely that you will be able consistently to identify the specific companies that will thrive, but we explain how to deal with that challenge elsewhere. What's important to focus on now is that stock prices, over time, reflect the ability of companies to make and distribute profits. Consider that stocks on average have returned about 6 percent a year over the past seven decades, adjusted for inflation. That figure didn't materialize by virtue of magic or voodoo. During the period in question, corporate profits rose an inflation-adjusted average of about 3 percent annually, while the average stock yielded roughly 3 percent a year in dividends. From these numbers does the 6 percent figure arise. Of course, in the short run stock prices may rise for reasons having little to do with dividends or profitability—as investors in high-flying Internet stocks happily know. But, again, over long periods of time it has been proven that share prices rise in relation to companies' earnings and distribution of profits to shareholders.

None of the above, by the way, is meant to imply that stocks should be your *only* investment. It's wise to spread your wealth among a variety of asset classes, including stocks, bonds, real estate, cash, and maybe even gold. But if you don't plan to start tapping your long-term savings for at least five years, stocks should probably constitute the bulk of your portfolio, depending on your ability to tolerate the ups and downs of the stock market. Even folks who draw current income from their investments—retirees, for example—should probably have a portion of their savings in stocks so that their money will grow faster than inflation.

Focus on the big picture. For diversification to work as a salve for the pains of loss, you must avoid looking at losses or gains in isolation. You have to train yourself to view your individual investments as parts of a broader whole. This takes discipline. It's not easy for anyone to say, "Hey, my U.S. stock mutual fund dropped 10 percent, but at least my European bonds went up 8 percent." That's why it's often helpful to invest in a spreadsheet computer program such as Excel, or a software package like Quicken, that can display and total all your investments.

It's also important, however distasteful the task may be, to spend time developing a concrete investment philosophy and strategy and to put it down on paper. For example, determine the portion of your portfolio that should be invested in stocks, bonds, real estate, and cash. Then write it down, with a notation as to when that allocation should be reexamined (perhaps as you approach your goal). You might also write down the specific investing rationale for each of your investments. That will serve as a reminder to hang tight if the price drops ("Coke is still the most popular brand name in the world") or to sell if need be ("Asia's economies might not be as strong as I thought when I invested in the Thai Fund").

Writing things down, we've found, raises the "ante" and increases your commitment. In fact, it's a way of using the sunk cost fallacy to your advantage, because by increasing your investment in taking a broad view of your wealth (by investing time and effort in the task), you'll increase the likelihood that you'll stick to your plans. In any event, if you take such an approach—identifying your goals and justifying all your investments in the context of achieving those goals—you'll be less likely to react impulsively to the inevitable ups and downs of the markets.

Forget the past. We don't want to sound too new age here, but very often our decisions about the future are weighed down by our actions of the past. People stay in unsatisfying careers because of the time and money they invested in school, not because they enjoy the work or expect to in the future; we finish a bad book because we've already gotten so far, not because we're anxious to see how the characters live; we sit through a boring movie because we bought the ticket, not because it's a good flick. The same motivations affect our decisions about money: We spend more money on car repairs because we've already spent so much on the car; we keep spending money on tennis lessons because we've already spent so much. We hold on to bad investments because we can't get over how much we paid for them and can't bear to make that bad investment "final."

Well, get over it.

No, we're not trying to be harsh. If we could, we'd send you a pill that erases the memory of every dollar you ever spent (except, perhaps, when filling out expense reports and tax returns). That's because once spent, it's gone. It has no relevance (except maybe for refunds). To the extent that you can incorporate that notion into your financial decisions, you'll be that much better off for trying. If you're debating the sale of an investment (or a home), for example, remember that your goal is to maximize your wealth and your enjoyment. *The goal is not to justify your decision to buy the investment at whatever price you originally paid for it.* Who cares? What counts, in terms of getting where you want to be tomorrow, is what that investment is worth today. That's why you must evaluate all investments (and expenses) based on their *current* potential for future loss and future gain.

How does one go about forgetting the past? One helpful device we like is a method of reframing decisions to remove emotional investments. We call it "pressing the rewind button." Assume that you can reverse history and start anew. Here's how this might work.

Imagine that you've got a ten-year-old minivan that needs a new transmission. The sunk cost fallacy tells us that you're more likely to plunk down the money for the new transmission if you've recently sunk hundreds or thousands on repairs into your clunker before that. So ask yourself: If someone gave you the minivan as a gift yesterday, would you spend the money today to get it running? If the answer is "no"—because that large an investment is not worth it on its merit—then it's probably time to think about buying a new car. Similarly, it is relevant only to your ego that your Amalgamated Thingamabobs stock, for which you paid $100 a share, is now selling for $25 a share. If you believe that lower price is a bargain, hold on and maybe even buy more shares. But if it is not—if, given the chance, you would pass on the opportunity to buy the same shares at any price today—then it is time to sell. So ask yourself when evaluating investments: "Would I buy this today, at this price?" If not, you may not want to own it any longer.

Reframe losses as gains. We're not suggesting that you dump every losing stock or mutual fund or other security that you might own. Sometimes investments fall in price; if the economy is in the tank, only lucky investors manage to avoid temporary declines in their portfolio. So, again, each of your investments must be evaluated individually and with an eye on your financial situation. However, once you have identified assets that need to be dumped, you might still find it difficult to do so, to make the loss real and final.

One way to hop this hurdle is to turn the loss into a gain, and the easiest way to do that is to remember that selling investments at a loss creates a tax-deductible event: Losses on investments that you've held for less than twelve months can be written off against capital gains; losses on investments held longer than twelve months can be deducted from ordinary income. By viewing your potential loss as a gain—the gain being the lower amount of taxes you'll owe—you master your own mental tendencies. Need an example? Say you bought one hundred shares of Amalgamated Thingamabobs three years ago for $100 a share, or $10,000. If you sell today at $70 a share—for a total loss of $3,000—and you're in the 28 percent federal tax bracket, your loss is actually worth $840 to you. If that isn't a kind of gain, we don't know what is!

Use Weber's law to your advantage. Recall that the change in any stimulus matters less and less with every increase in the absolute level of that stimulus. That's why adding five pounds to a fifteen-pound dumbbell matters a lot, but the same addition to a two-hundred-pound barbell is hardly noticed. It also explains why a $1 increase in the hourly wage you are paid for a part-time job at the bowling alley seems more significant than the same increase in the (presumably higher) hourly wage you're paid for your day job. What this means is that to stretch your enjoyment from the good things in life, you should "segregate gains" whenever possible. Spread them out. You would not want to receive both your state and federal tax refunds on the same day, for example, because you would doubtless combine them mentally into one overall windfall and thus diminish your enjoyment. The pleasure you experience from receiving, say, $1,000 on one day would be less than what you would derive from getting $700 one week and $300 the next.

Of course, you cannot determine exactly when your tax refunds will arrive. But you can time many of life's windfalls, and when you can, spread them out. The same logic, of course, implies that you will be better off if you "integrate losses." If you have a number of cavities to be filled, get them all taken care of in one trip to the dentist. Don't subject yourself to multiple traumas by having a few filled on one visit and the rest on another. Weber's law implies that the pain of two moderately bad experiences will typically exceed the pain of experiencing both at one time. If you *owe* the government money, then you should pay your state and federal taxes at the same time.

Finally, pay less attention to your investments. Horrors! How can we think such heresy? Don't worry, we're not advocating turning a totally blind eye to your hard-earned savings, mostly because nobody would listen: a recent American Stock Exchange study indicates that nearly 40 percent of young, middle-class investors check their investment returns *once a week!* And that's simply too often. The more frequently you check your investments, the more you'll notice—and feel the urge to react to—the ups and downs that are an inevitable part of the stock and bond markets. For most investors —frankly, for all investors who don't trade professionally—a yearly review of your portfolio is frequent enough to make necessary adjustments in your allocation of assets. True, you might miss a market dip or rise when the chairman of the Federal Reserve sneezes or smiles. Which means, come to think of it, that you might miss an opportunity to let your psyche get in the way of your financial peace of mind.

CHAPTER 3

THE DEVIL THAT YOU KNOW

I went down to the crossroads. Fell down on my knees.
—From Robert Johnson's "Crossroads," made famous by the 1960s rock group Cream

If you choose not to decide, you still have made a choice.
—From "Free Will," by the 1970s rock group Rush

When it comes to finances, there are not only sins of commission, but sins of omission as well. In practice, some of the more serious and costly financial mistakes people make are the result of inaction. It's not always what you do that hurts your pocketbook, but what you choose not to do. To understand why people decide not to decide —or, more accurately, why people resist change—we will return once again to Daniel Kahneman and Amos Tversky's spadework. Prospect theory, as we saw earlier, helps explain how loss aversion, and an inability to ignore sunk costs, leads people to take actions that are not in their best interest. The sting of losing money, for example, often leads investors to pull money out of the stock market unwisely when prices dip. Similarly, it leads car owners to pay for expensive repairs because of money already spent on previous fixes.

Both examples, however, demonstrate how loss aversion and the sunk cost fallacy often lead us to *take* action—to actually *do* something. But prospect theory also explains how those very same tendencies can lead us to avoid or delay action. Indeed, loss aversion and several other factors —particularly the fear of regret and a preference for the same old thing—contribute to a phenomenon that we like to call "decision paralysis," making the idea of many proactive decisions especially daunting and uncomfortable. So let's examine the way people reach decisions—how decisions are made generally and why you might decide "not to decide." Once you're familiar with the complicated forces at work, you'll better understand why choice and change can be so intimidating. It's a phenomenon that hampers people in all walks of life, from choosing a video rental to buying a house. Not surprisingly, the higher the stakes, the more conflicted we feel. And for most people, the stakes are never higher than they are when the choices involve their finances.

EENY, MEENY, MINY, MO . . .

Imagine that you're considering the purchase of a compact disc player, but as yet you haven't decided which brand or model you want, or even how much you want to spend. Walking past an electronics store one day, you notice a sign in the window advertising a popular Sony CD *player that's on sale for $99. You know this price to be well below retail. Would you:*

1. *buy the Sony?*
2. *wait to learn more about other models?*

Now imagine the same situation, except that the store is also advertising a high-quality Aiwa disc player for $159. As with the Sony, you know the price for the Aiwa to be a bargain. Would you:

1. *buy the Aiwa?*
2. *buy the Sony?*
3. *wait to learn more about other models?*

A funny thing happened when Tversky and Princeton University psychologist Eldar Shafir presented one of these two hypotheticals to two different groups of students at Stanford and Princeton. The overwhelming majority of one group, which was presented with only the first scenario, said they would buy the Sony, while roughly a third said they would wait and shop some more. The decision to buy makes sense, given that the price on the Sony was obviously a good deal and given the presumption that the students were on the prowl for a CD player anyway. Meanwhile, when the other group of students was presented with the second situation, slightly more than one in four (27 percent) said they would buy the Sony, while a like amount said they would buy the Aiwa. *This time, though, nearly half of the students (46 percent) said they wouldn't do anything;* they'd wait to see what else was out there. Note the irony here: The addition of a second "good deal" from which to choose makes people less likely to take advantage of either opportunity.

At one level, the conclusion to be reached from this and similar experiments is not surprising: The more choices people face in life, the more likely they are to simply do nothing. But Tversky and

Shafir also found that diversity of choice alone was not the determining factor in the students' decision to put off buying a CD player once the number of choices increased. They showed that was *not* the case in another experiment, in which another group of students was presented with a scenario similar to our second one, except that the Aiwa was replaced by a noticeably less appealing brand of CD player. In this instance—another case of two buying options from which to choose—only one in four students said they would wait to make a purchase.

What Tversky and Shafir realized in formulating their theory of "choice under conflict" is that a decision to delay an action, or take no action at all, becomes more likely when there are many attractive options from which to choose. Consider a study conducted by psychologists Sheena Sethi and Mark Lepper at an upscale grocery store in Menlo Park, California. In catering to the refined tastes of its clientele, the store offers patrons 250 flavors of mustard, 75 different olive oils, and over 300 types of jam. The store also offered Sethi and Lepper the opportunity to conduct their clever field experiment by allowing them to set up a tasting booth in the store on two consecutive Saturdays. Every hour the two psychologists rotated what was available at the booth—one hour it was a selection of twenty-four different jams, and another hour it was a more limited selection of six. The two sets of jams were chosen carefully so that they were rated, on average, by an independent sample of tasters to be equally delicious. Anyone who approached the booth during the course of the study was given a coupon good for $1 off any jam in the store. The bar code written on each coupon also contained information specifying whether the customer had approached the booth when it displayed six or twenty-four jams.

The two psychologists were interested to learn whether customers who were exposed to a set of twenty-four jams would be so befuddled by all the options that they would not be able to decide which to buy and thus be less likely to make a purchase than those exposed to the more limited set of six jams. The bar codes, of course, made it a simple matter to keep track. And, in fact, customers who had seen fewer jams did buy more. Although more people visited the booth when it contained the rather dazzling array of twenty-four jams (by a 145–104 margin), 30 percent of those exposed to the set of six subsequently made a purchase, whereas only 3 percent of those exposed to the set of twenty-four did so. The more choice, in other words, the harder the choice.

Such findings may seem like common sense, but their ramifications throughout society reverberate wide and deep. Indeed, we suspect that choice conflict is one of the reasons "progress"—defined in late twentieth-century America as the freedom to choose from an ever expanding selection of products, services, and opportunities—seems to engender as much angst as it does excitement. We may think we want nearly unlimited selections of televisions, or vacations, or jobs. But in some immeasurable way, this exploding freedom of choice raises its own discomfort and difficulties, particularly when the choices are good and getting better.

But enough contemplation about the impact of consumerism on the meaning of life. Let's move on to money. One important result of decision paralysis in financial decisions is that by deferring purchasing decisions, you may miss a sale entirely or run the risk that prices will rise. How many tales have you heard—or lived through—in which Jane and John Homebuyer couldn't pull the trigger on their dream house, only to see the price go up when another bidder entered the game? Of greater concern, however, is the choice conflict brought on by the plethora of investment options available to Americans today.

It's ironic that one of the most significant developments in the "democratization" of wealth in this country—the explosive growth of mutual funds and the increasing prevalence of defined contribution retirement plans—is also a cause of tremendous money anguish. Today there are more than 6,800 publicly traded stock and bond funds, and for many people, the prospect of choosing among them is paralyzing.

This paralysis is inflicted in several ways, both obvious and subtle. First and most obvious, decision paralysis is certainly one of the culprits responsible for the $1.2 trillion that Americans have stashed in bank passbook savings and money market accounts. Yes, some of that money needs to be highly liquid, and yes, federally insured bank deposits are about the safest investment extant today. But liquidity and surety cannot be the only reason for such a high level of bank deposits. After all, money market mutual funds typically offer yields that are twice those paid by banks, and with nearly as much safety. For example, a money market fund that invests only in U.S. Treasury securities is about as safe—and accessible—a place to stash money as a bank that is insured by the Federal Deposit Insurance Corporation. But choosing a money market fund in which to invest among the hundreds of available options means making a choice between a number of seemingly equal and excellent choices (along with a lot of bad ones, too). And for many people, that is a very intimidating task.

Similarly, decision paralysis helps to explain why so many people fail to make appropriate investment decisions in employee-directed retirement plans, such as 401(k), 403(b), and 457 accounts. Faced with a choice between, say, several international and domestic stock funds and several high-yielding fixed-income products, many people choose the equivalent of a wait-and-see default option: they allocate all their money to the most conservative investment available on the theory that at some point they'll get around to figuring out what they should do. Or, having initially chosen among a few options when they first joined a retirement plan, many employees balk at changing their initial selections even when new and potentially better options are introduced.

Such intransigence is a mistake on two counts. First, tax-deferred retirement accounts are the very portfolios where the risks of investing in stocks are most mitigated: who cares if the short-term value of your 401(k) account goes up and down with the stock market? By the time you'll need the money—presuming you have at least ten years until retirement—chances are that the roller-coaster nature of equities will be a memory. What you'll have left is a large pot of money, assuming you take advantage of the historically high returns that stocks have posted in comparison with bonds and other types of investments. So the longer you let decision paralysis contribute to procrastination—the longer you defer choice—the greater the chance that you'll miss out on the heady returns that stocks offer.

More important, the longer you defer making a decision, the less likely you are to ever get over your hesitation. To illustrate this point, Tversky and Shafir offered students a $5 reward for answering and returning a long survey. One group was given five days to complete the survey, another group was given twenty-one days, and a third set of students was given no deadline at all. The result: Sixty-six percent of the first group (five-day deadline) turned in the survey and collected the reward, 40 percent of the second group (twenty-one days) finished on time, and 25 percent of the third group (no deadline) had turned in their questionnaire by the time the researchers stopped calculating. Now, maybe students in that last group are still planning to collect their $5, but we doubt it. The reality is that the more time you have to do a task—any task

—the less pressure you feel to "get with it," and the frequent result is that you never get to it at all. Such delays, needless to say, can be costly.

THE CHOICE IS YOURS (SORT OF)

Indecision is typically overcome, not surprisingly, when people feel they have sound reasons for choosing one option over another. What could be more sensible? It turns out, however, that the search for decisive reasons can make people vulnerable to psychological tendencies of which they are unaware. Tversky and Itamar Simonson, then an assistant professor in the business school at the University of California at Berkeley, demonstrated the impact of several of these tendencies in a 1992 paper in the *Journal of Marketing Research.*

In one experiment people were given pictures and descriptions of five microwave ovens taken from a popular catalog. After studying the offerings carefully—which you might want to do, too, since it's a bit confusing—half of the participants were asked to choose among two of these products: a 0.5-cubic-foot Emerson microwave, on sale for 35 percent off its $109.99 retail price; and a 0.8-cubic-foot Panasonic I oven, selling for 35 percent off its $179.99 price. As it happened, 57 percent chose the Emerson, *while 43 percent favored the Panasonic I.* Meanwhile another group of participants was given three ovens from which to choose—the two already mentioned and a 1.1-cubic-foot Panasonic II, selling for 10 percent off its $199.99 price. Interestingly, the inclusion of a second Panasonic, which wasn't nearly as good a bargain as either of the other two, had the effect of increasing the number of people who now favored the Panasonic I. *Some 60 percent chose the Panasonic I,* while 27 percent chose the Emerson and 13 percent chose the Panasonic II.

Tversky and Simonson explain this as an example of "trade-off contrast," whereby choices are enhanced or hindered by the trade-offs between options—even those we wouldn't choose anyway. In other words, when the Panasonic I was compared with the Emerson alone, few people had a decisive reason to choose one over the other; it was a trade-off between size (Panasonic) and price (Emerson). However, when the Panasonic II was introduced into the mix, the Panasonic I now had a couple of things going for it: its size was adequate, and it could be had for a good price (35 percent off, as opposed to the 10 percent savings on the Panasonic II). The Panasonic I thus became a better deal—not only versus its pricier cousin, but also in comparison with the Emerson. Consider it this way: If A (the Emerson) is better than B (the Panasonic I), people will generally choose A. But if B happens to be better than C (the Panasonic II) in ways that are not applicable to A, many people will now choose B if for no other reason than B's appeal has been enhanced by comparison with C.

Another intriguing phenomenon was revealed in a related experiment in which Tversky and Simonson offered one group of participants a choice between 2 thirty-five-millimeter cameras—a Minolta X-370 priced at $169.99 and a Minolta Maxxum 3000i selling for $239.99. The preferred choice? An even split—50 percent chose each model. Meanwhile a second group of participants was offered a choice of the same two cameras as well as a Minolta Maxxum 7000I selling for $469.99. You might expect that however many opted for the new model, the remaining people would again split their choices relatively evenly between the two cheaper models. Not so. Instead the medium-priced camera was now preferred over the cheaper model by more than a two-to-one margin. Tversky and Simonson call this phenomenon "extremeness aversion." Stated simply, people are more likely to choose an option if it is an intermediate choice within a group, rather than at one extreme end. The X-370, for example, was the choice of half the study subjects when it was one of two options, but the choice of little more than a fifth when it was at one end of the spectrum.

Evidence of both these tendencies abound in real life, but one of the most egregious and costly examples occurs when people are at their most vulnerable—when buying coffins, which range in cost from less than $500 to $70,000! It's common practice within the funeral industry to show bereaved relatives a selection of caskets designed specifically to 1) highlight the enhancements of more expensive caskets in comparison with cheaper ones; and 2) ignore or replace lower-priced caskets in the "showroom." To illustrate this point, we quote from a 1996 *Time* magazine story about a Vancouver, Canada, "death care" company, the Loewen Group: "Loewen also institutes its 'Third Unit Target Merchandising' system in the casket showroom, which capitalizes on the propensity of survivors to avoid the cheapest two caskets and choose the next one up in price. 'It's no different from any other business operating a showroom,' says Lawrence Millers, president of Loewen's cemetery division. But often, two former officials agree, *this means banishing a newly acquired home's usual lowest-price offerings and replacing them with more expensive substitutes,* so that when the customer picks that third-unit target, he ends up choosing a casket that yields a much better profit." (our italics)

KNOWN QUANTITIES

A close cousin to decision paralysis is resistance to change. That is, people are almost preternaturally predisposed to the familiar, to keeping things much as they have been. Behavioral economists call this the "status quo bias," and it has been demonstrated numerous times. One of the most compelling of these demonstrations was a series of studies conducted by William Samuelson of Boston University and Richard Zeckhauser of Harvard University. In one experiment, individuals with a working knowledge of economics and finance were presented with a problem much like the following:

You are a serious reader of the financial pages, but until recently you have had little money to invest. Now a great-uncle has bequeathed to you a large sum of money. In considering how to invest these funds, you have narrowed down your choices to the following four investment options:

1. Shares of XYZ Incorporated, a stock of moderate risk with a 50 percent chance that over the next year its price will increase by 30 percent, a 20 percent chance that it will stay the same, and a 30 percent chance that it will decline 20 percent.

2. Shares of ABC Incorporated, a more risky stock with a 40 percent chance that over the next year its price will double, a 30 percent chance that it will stay the same, and a 30 percent chance that it will decline 40 percent.

3. U.S. Treasury bills, with an almost certain return of 9 percent over the next year.

4. Municipal bonds, with an almost certain return over the next year of 6 percent, tax-free.

Which option would you choose?

As you might expect, the students in this study selected one or another of the investment options depending on their willingness to take risk. Thus 32 percent opted for the moderately risky stock investment, 32 percent opted for the conservative municipal bond option, 18 percent opted for the risky stock investment, and another 18 percent opted for the T-bills. Those results, however, were not especially important, surprising, or interesting on their own. The good stuff came when Samuelson and Zeckhauser offered other groups of students a similar problem, except that for each of these other groups a status quo was established. That is, each one of the groups was told that an investment decision had already been made, and they were now being asked if they wanted to stay where they were or if they wanted to switch to another option. For example, one such alternative scenario went something like this:

You are a serious reader of the financial pages, but until recently you have had little money to invest. A while back, however, a great-uncle bequeathed to you a large sum of money, a significant portion of which is now invested in the shares of XYZ Incorporated. Now you must decide whether to leave the portfolio as is or change it by investing it elsewhere. You have no concern about the tax and brokerage commissions. Which option would you choose?

1. Retain the shares of XYZ Incorporated, a stock of moderate risk with a 50 percent chance that over the next year its price will increase by 30 percent, a 20 percent chance that it will stay the same, and a 30 percent chance that it will decline 20 percent.

2. Invest in shares of ABC Incorporated, a more risky stock with a 40 percent chance that over the next year its price will double, a 30 percent chance that it will stay the same, and a 30 percent chance that it will decline 40 percent.

3. Invest in U.S. Treasury bills, with an almost certain return of 9 percent over the next year.

4. Invest in municipal bonds, with an almost certain return over the next year of 6 percent, tax-free.

And the results of these experiments? No matter which investment option was presented as the status quo, it was the favorite choice of subjects in each group. So, for example, 47 percent of the people who were told that they were already invested in municipal bonds chose to stay with these very conservative investments, compared with just 32 percent who chose them when none of the four options was described as the default option, or status quo. Ponder this for a moment: When all things were equal, only three in ten people chose munis as their preferred investment. Yet once they were told that they already owned these securities—even though they had not chosen that investment themselves—nearly half the people decided that munis were the way to go.

This is a classic example of the status quo bias. But the question begging for an answer, of course, is "Why?" Why are people so resistant to change, so intent on not rocking the boat? More to the point: Is there something so intrinsically attractive about the status quo? Or is there something inherently frightening about the prospect of change? The answer to both questions, as you will understand in a moment, is a definitive "yes."

WHAT'S MINE IS MINE, AND WHAT'S YOURS ISN'T WORTH AS MUCH

Imagine that you recently found a ticket to the most prestigious inaugural ball of the recently elected U.S. president. You very much want to attend. Now a stranger offers to buy your precious ticket. What is the smallest amount for which you would sell?

Now imagine that you don't have a ticket to the ball, but you really want one. How much would you pay that same stranger for his?

If you think about it, the status quo bias is in part a measure of satisfaction. By forgoing change in favor of the familiar, you are to some extent demonstrating a level of happiness with your present situation. True, the decision to invest or not, to spend or not, or to marry or not may be influenced by fear, confusion, or doubt. Nonetheless, keeping things as they are is a vote of confidence for current circumstances, however weakly that vote may be cast. In fact, the preference for "holding on to what you got" is a lot stronger than most people think. People tend to overvalue what belongs to them relative to the value they would place on the same possession or circumstance if it belonged to someone else.

Behavioral economists call this the "endowment effect," and it helps to explain why most people would demand at least twice as much to *sell* the aforementioned ticket to the inaugural ball than they would to *buy* it. Richard Thaler demonstrated the endowment effect in a series of experiments several years ago. In one of them, half the students in a Cornell economics class were given a mug emblazoned with the school's logo. The mug, which sold at the campus bookstore for $6, was examined by all the students—those who had just received them as a gift and those who hadn't. Given that the mugs were handed out randomly, it is unlikely that those who received the free mugs loved coffee (or Cornell) more than the students who did not. Thaler then conducted an auction of sorts to see how much money the mug owners would require to part with their ceramic cups and how much the students who didn't have mugs would pay to own one.

You can probably guess what happened: The median price below which mug owners were *unwilling to sell* was $5.25, on average. That is, they wouldn't give up their newfound possession for less than that amount. Conversely, the median price above which mug buyers were *unwilling* to pay was about $2.75. That is, they wouldn't pay more than that amount to buy a mug. (The Cornell Campus Store is obviously not targeting students—economics students, at any rate—with its $6 mugs!) The only way to explain this discrepancy is the endowment effect. The mere fact of ownership was enough to make mug owners value a pretty basic campus commodity almost twice as much as did students who didn't own the mugs. And remember, there was no sunk cost effect at work here; no money had been spent on these mugs.

Because people place an inordinately high value on what they have, decisions to change become all the more difficult. To be sure, people manage to overcome this tendency all the time. If they didn't, folks wouldn't sell their homes, divorce their spouses, or trade in used cars for new ones. But to the extent that the endowment effect makes it hard to properly value what is—and isn't—already yours, you may fail to pursue options that are in your best interest. In essence, the endowment effect is really just another manifestation of loss aversion: people place too much emphasis on their out-of-pocket expenses (what they have to pay now) and too little value on opportunity costs (what they miss by not taking an action).

A FOOT IN THE DOOR

Businesses understand the endowment effect all too well. That's why so many manufacturers and retailers offer trial periods and money-back guarantees on purchases. Oriental carpet dealers are especially noted for this practice, but it is common in many industries. Store owners and other marketers understand that once you take a product home and use it, there's a strong chance that the endowment effect will kick in. Whatever value you might have placed on, say, a stereo at a store will likely be increased once it sits in your den for a few weeks. Remember that the next time you consider trying out a product because you can "always return it." Maybe you can, and maybe you can't.

One of the most costly and regrettable examples of how the endowment effect leads people to ignore opportunity costs occurs in connection with retirement savings plans at work. First, a little background. Some 29 million U.S. workers are eligible to participate in 401(k) retirement plans, which (as you may very well know) are tax-deferred savings vehicles funded mostly by workers themselves. However, the typical employer matches fifty cents to each dollar contributed by plan participants, up to 6 percent of the employee's salary. In other words, someone who makes $50,000 a year and contributes $3,000 will receive an extra $1,500 from his or her boss. That's right: $1,500 *free of charge.* But according to a 1996 survey by Buck Consultants, roughly 12 million people a year who are eligible for this free money choose not to accept it, either because they don't contribute to their 401(k) plan at all or because they don't contribute enough to qualify for a full employer match.

Certainly some people fail to contribute because they don't know how the plans work or because they absolutely cannot spare a dime from their salary for their retirement. Mostly, though, this mistake —which, according to a *Money* magazine estimate, costs employees $6 billion a year in missed employer matches—can be blamed on loss aversion and the endowment effect. Parting with money today is experienced as a loss, or out-of-pocket cost, and is therefore hard to do. At the same time, the future benefits from doing so are experienced as foregone gains and therefore relatively easy to ignore. Stated differently, people overvalue what they have (today's salary) and fail to properly value what they could have (the employee matches and the benefits of tax-deferred savings).

ANYTHING BUT SORRY

Suppose Fred owns $1,000 worth of stock in General Motors. A trusted friend suggests that Fred sell it and buy $1,000 of Ford stock. Fred does not sell, and over the next year GM's share price drops 30 percent, turning his $1,000 holding into a $700 investment.

Now suppose that Wilma owns $1,000 worth of Ford stock. During the same period, a trusted friend of hers suggests that she sell her shares and buy $1,000 worth of GM. She does this, and over the next year GM's share price drops 30 percent, turning Wilma's $1,000 investment into a $700 investment stake in GM.

Who do you think feels worse, Fred or Wilma?

The last piece of the puzzle that we call decision paralysis is a concept that may be the easiest to understand, given its everyday emotional resonance. In many ways it is a concept that envelops much of prospect theory and its attendant tendencies—loss aversion, the status quo bias, and the endowment effect. The idea—which behavioral economists call "regret aversion"—is as simple as it sounds. Most people want to avoid the pain of regret and the responsibility for negative outcomes. And to the extent that decisions to act—decisions to change the status quo—impart a higher level of responsibility than decisions to do nothing, people are naturally averse to sticking their necks out and setting themselves up for feelings of regret.

That's why most people, when evaluating whether Fred or Wilma feels worse about the decline in GM's stock price, assume that Wilma would be more unhappy than Fred. After all, Wilma took action that resulted in her losing money, while Fred did nothing—or at least seemed to do nothing. There's no question that both investors probably feel lousy, but the assumption is that Wilma will kick herself harder. She is likely to castigate herself with thoughts of "This need not have happened" or "I brought this on myself." And that feeling of regret is one that people will often go to great lengths to avoid.

They might even pay for it. Richard Thaler, in a 1980 paper published in the *Journal of Economic Behavior and Organization,* offered the following hypothetical to make the point:

Mr. A. is waiting in line at a movie theater. When he gets to the ticket window he is told that as the one hundred thousandth customer of the theater, he has just won $100.

Mr. B is waiting in line at a different theater. The man in front of him wins $1,000 for being the one millionth customer of the theater. Mr. B wins $150.

Who would you rather be, Mr. A or Mr. B?

Incredibly, writes Thaler, many people would actually prefer Mr. A's position (up $100) to that of Mr. B (up $150)! The reason is regret aversion. These souls would feel so bad about missing out on the $1,000 prize that they would effectively pay $50 to avoid regret over having been a step late to the theater.

This probably isn't too surprising. Knowingly or not, you probably pay good money all the time to avoid feelings of regret or to otherwise maintain the status quo. Leaving money in a bank account rather than putting the cash in an investment with a higher return; staying in a relatively low-paying job rather than making a switch to one with a higher salary; failing to sell an investment only to see it drop in price; delaying a purchase only to see the price rise; keeping revolving balances on a high-rate credit card rather than switching to one with lower finance charges: all of these inactions are examples of the ways that regret aversion, decision paralysis, and the status quo bias combine to influence your financial decisions and to cost you money.

One last thought about regret. The claim that people have a particularly acute fear of regrettable action may not feel right to you. Your own biggest regrets, for example, may involve things you have failed to do. Or you may recall the words of John Greenleaf Whittier who wrote, "For of all sad words of tongue or pen, the saddest are these: 'It might have been!' " A valid point, to be sure. In fact, Tom has conducted research indicating that most people's biggest regrets in life do indeed center around things they have failed to do. Not spending enough time with the kids. Not taking a career more seriously. Not reconciling with a now departed relative. But note that these regrets take time to develop and are quite unlike the pain of losing money by switching one stock for another, a pain that descends immediately. Tom's research indicates that people experience more regret over their mistakes of action in the short term, while regrets of inaction are the ones that are more painful in the long run. The evidence thus reinforces the wisdom of Mark Twain, who said, "Twenty years from now you will be more disappointed by the things you didn't do than by the ones you did do."

HOW TO THINK AND WHAT TO DO

WARNING SIGNS

You might suffer from decision paralysis if . . .

- you have a hard time choosing among investment options.
- you don't contribute to retirement plans at work.
- you tend to beat yourself up when your decisions turn out poorly.
- you frequently buy things that offer "trial periods"—but infrequently take advantage and return them.
- you delay making investment or spending decisions.

We need to be careful in offering advice on how to deal with decision paralysis. After all, caution can be as much a positive force in your life as a negative influence, if it keeps you from making unwise decisions rather than beneficial ones. Only *you* can determine if an inability to "pull the trigger" on decisions costs or saves you money. However, if you perceive choice conflict as a problem for you, here are five helpful ideas to keep in mind:

Remember: Deciding not to decide is a decision. Postponement, delay, procrastination. They may seem like the path of least resistance, but they are in their own way as consequential as any other choice, a sort of passive-aggressive approach to decision making. Every instance when you decide to maintain the status quo is really a vote of confidence for the way you've been doing things. Is that confidence warranted?

Don't forget opportunity costs. Gary's former colleague at *Money*, the mutual fund writer Jason Zweig, likes to remind people that someone who invested in a lousy stock mutual fund fifteen years ago—and stuck with it—is probably better off today than someone who didn't invest in stocks at all. Our point here is this: Even if a financial decision is not perfect (most are not), it may still leave you in a better position than if you had done nothing. When contemplating financial decisions, you are more than likely to pay too much attention to what you have now than what you might have down the road. And because of the status quo bias and regret aversion, you are more likely to focus on the ways in which your decision to spend or invest can make you feel bad for having undertaken change.

To combat these tendencies, imagine how you'd feel if a proactive step you are considering worked out—but you didn't take the chance. Think how you would feel if that investment rose in price as you thought it might, or if the price of that stereo went up 10 percent by the time you realized that you really do want better sound quality. The imaginary feelings of regret you may conjure up could help you overcome your real-life resistance to change.

Put yourself on autopilot. Instead of having to make an endless series of decisions about whether now is a good time to invest, use "dollar cost averaging." This is a strategy that involves investing a set amount of money at regular intervals in a stock or bond or mutual fund—regardless of whether the markets are rising or falling. In this way you end up buying fewer shares when the price of an investment is high and more when the price is lower. Similarly, people who have trouble controlling their spending can have their mortgage payment—most any payment, really—deducted from their bank account so they'll never have to "choose" between making a loan payment or spending that money on something else.

Play your own devil's advocate. A simple way to make decisions more easily is to change your frame of reference. One method we have found helpful is to approach decisions from a neutral state. In other words, force yourself to imagine that you're starting from ground zero rather than from a status quo position. For example, in the Ford/General Motors scenario mentioned earlier, Fred probably approached his choice as a decision to stick with or abandon his stock in GM. A more helpful way to have evaluated his choice would be to imagine that his money was invested in neither stock. His decision would then be this: In which automobile maker do I want to invest, Ford or GM? In most cases such an approach would allow Fred to evaluate the two companies on their merits, rather than weighting the evaluation in favor of GM because it occupied the status quo position.

Another way to alter your decision-making frame is to reverse the context in which you perceive the choice at hand. In other words, turn a decision of which option to reject into one of which option to select, and vice versa. This should help you focus on both the positive and the negative attributes of your options, rather than give disproportionate weight to one or the other. For example, if you're deciding among investment options and you find yourself unable to choose which one you prefer, ask yourself instead which options you would (in no instance) choose. Or, assume instead that you already own all of the choices. Now your decision becomes which one to sell—which ones you definitely do not want to own. This may sound simple, and it should. The hard part is recognizing that your decision is being hampered by the way you're viewing the problem to begin with.

CHAPTER 4

NUMBER NUMBNESS

In a memorable episode of *The Simpsons,* Homer's boss, Mr. Burns, desperately wants his plant's softball team to defeat the squad of his rival. To aid in that effort, he hires a sports psychologist, who hypnotizes Homer's team in an attempt to extract maximum performance.

Psychologist: "You are all very good players."

Team (in trancelike tones): "We are all very good players."

Psychologist: "You will beat Shelbyville."

Team: "We will beat Shelbyville."

Psychologist: "You will give 110 percent."

Team (still in trance): "That's impossible. No one can give more than 100 percent. By definition, that is the most anyone can give."

We trust that the reader is every bit as savvy as Homer and his teammates and is thus annoyed by sportscasters who mention athletes whose efforts exceed 100 percent. Nevertheless, the episode does illustrate an important truism about the human condition—people have trouble with numbers. And although you doubtless did well on this particular example, there are some surprising facts about mathematics that confound just about everyone. Of course, we're not the first to reach this conclusion. In his wonderful book *Innumeracy: Mathematical Illiteracy and Its Consequences,* mathematician John Allen Paulos notes that "some of the blocks to dealing comfortably with numbers and probabilities are due to quite natural psychological responses to uncertainty, to coincidence, or to how a problem is framed. Others can be attributed to anxiety, or to romantic misconceptions about the nature and importance of mathematics." Our task here is to explain how innumeracy—defined by *Webster's* as an "ignorance of mathematics"—has practical and negative consequences for your finances, and to show how you can avoid them. We'll do that by focusing on three issues, though we could probably fill a book about the ways in which ignorance of numbers can affect (and afflict) your life.

The first issue is the tendency to ignore inflation, thanks to a psychological phenomenon known as "the money illusion." Next we'll have some fun with probabilities, and we'll show how failing to understand the role of odds and chance in life can lead you to make unwise investment and spending decisions. Finally we'll tackle what, for lack of a better phrase, we call the "bigness bias," or the way in which indifference to small numbers can cost big bucks, especially over time.

HOME AT LAST

In three successive years, Peter, Paul, and Mary each bought a home that cost $200,000, and each ended up selling their home one year later. During Peter's year of homeownership, the country experienced a period of 25 percent deflation—that is, the average price of all goods and services in the United States fell by 25 percent—and Peter sold his house for $154,000, or 23 percent less than he paid. During the twelve months that Paul owned his home, the situation was reversed: the average cost of goods and services actually rose 25 percent, and Paul eventually sold his home for $246,000, or 23 percent more than he paid. As for Mary, the cost of living during her year-long stretch of owning a home stayed pretty much the same, but she ended up selling her house for $196,000, or 2 percent less than she paid. Soon after, the three friends met for a drink, but their bonhomie ended in anger when they couldn't agree on the answer to what seemed a simple question: Factoring in the changes in overall consumer prices, which of the three came out the best in their home sales?

Not sure yourself who fared best? Not quite sure you even want to figure it out? Several years ago Princeton's Eldar Shafir conducted a study in which participants were presented with just such a story and then asked to evaluate how each seller fared—relative to each other and keeping in mind the state of the economy in general. Interestingly, a majority of the participants—about six in ten—thought Paul (who notched a 23 percent gain during a period when the average price of goods rose 25 percent) came out on top and Peter (a 23 percent loss, vs. a period when the average prices of goods *fell* 25 percent) fared worst. These majority conclusions are interesting, of course, because they're wrong. In reality, Peter made out much better. Indeed, he was the only homeowner who actually made money. When the rate of inflation is accounted for, he actually registered a 2 percent gain in buying power, while both Paul and Mary posted a 2 percent loss. In other words, although Paul received 23 percent more dollars for his home when he sold it than he paid for it, what those dollars could actually buy during his year of ownership declined by 25 percent. Peter, on the other hand, received 23 percent less upon selling than he'd shelled out a year earlier, but the overall decline in prices was actually 25 percent. Although one dollar's worth of goods or services last year could now be purchased for seventy-five cents, Peter received seventy-seven cents for every dollar he had spent on his home a year earlier. Peter's buying power, therefore, increased even as the average person's ability to pay for goods decreased.

By failing to understand this (admittedly complicated) distinction, the participants in Shafir's study fell victim to what behavioral economists call the "money illusion." This involves a confusion between "nominal" changes in money (greater or lesser numbers of actual dollars) and "real" changes (greater or lesser buying power) that reflect inflation or, more rarely these days, deflation. It's an understandable mistake, for a couple of reasons. First, accounting for inflation requires the application of a little arithmetic, which, as we've just discussed, is often an annoyance and downright impossible for many people. Second, inflation today, at least in the United States, is an incremental affair—2 percent to 4 percent, on average, over the past decade and a half. As we've touched upon already in our discussion of mental accounting in chapter 1—and as we'll delve into more deeply later in this chapter—little numbers are easy to discount or ignore. We suspect, though we don't know, that had Shafir conducted his study in certain Latin American or Eastern European countries, where double-digit or even triple-digit inflation has often been the norm, he might have found that participants were not as prone to the money illusion.

Nevertheless, most people we know routinely fail to consider the effects of inflation in their financial decision making, a gaffe that has myriad and negative short-term and long-term implications. For the moment, however, we'll focus on just three of them. First, the money illusion is dangerous because failing to grasp the effects of inflation may lead you to underestimate how much money will be required to meet future needs such as retirement or college. For example, a person who invests $10,000 today in the stock market will have about $67,000 in twenty years, assuming a 10 percent average annual return, whereas a person who invests $10,000 in U.S. Treasury bonds earning 6 percent a year will have about $32,000. Many people, of course, willingly give up the greater returns—and the ups and downs—of stocks in exchange for the ironclad security of government bonds. After all, $32,000 is still a lot of money—at least, that is, until inflation takes its toll. Consider: Assuming average annual price hikes of 4 percent, the stock investor would have the equivalent of $32,000 in today's money and buying power after two decades had passed. The bond investor, meanwhile, would have less than $15,000. That's the irony of a so-called conservative investment strategy: it is arguably more risky (and reckless) to leave yourself vulnerable to the ravages of inflation than it is to subject yourself to the hills and valleys of the stock market.

A related way in which the money illusion plays tricks with finances is by providing a false sense of history, a sort of 20/20 hindsight. Consider residential real estate. For longer than we can remember, a rule of thumb for home buyers has been to buy the biggest home possible—even if you have to stretch—on the logic that rising home prices will reward owners later with a tremendous return on their investment. But this bedrock belief that home values always appreciate—and that residential real estate is perhaps the best investment an individual can make—was crystallized during a relatively short but dramatic period in the late 1970s, when home prices skyrocketed. What most people forget or ignore, however, is that inflation during that period was soaring as well. Of course home prices were rising like soufflés; the price of everything was going through the roof. Once inflation was tamed, home prices have performed much as they always have: since 1980, for example, the median price for a U.S. home has risen 1.1 percent annually, after adjusting for inflation—vs. about 6 percent in inflation-adjusted terms for the U.S. stock market. Now, we're certainly not advising people to sell their home (or avoid buying one altogether) and pour *all* their money into the stock market. But to the extent that people have been counting on residential real estate to build household wealth, well, that's just another example of how the money illusion can cloud your vision and hurt your pocketbook.

Our final example of the deleterious effects of the money illusion is an example of how "inflation," in one form or another, can lead us to foolish or irrational behavior. This is just supposition, but we suspect that much of the wild swings of stock prices in recent years (and the media frenzy that seems to go along with them) is a direct result of the tremendous and breakneck pace of share price appreciation in recent years. Because stock prices have risen so steeply and so quickly in the last half of this decade—as opposed to the gradual rise over the previous twenty-five years—most investors (professional and amateur) have not adjusted their psychology to account for seemingly larger swings in prices. That is, in 1987 a two hundred-point swing in the Dow Jones Industrial Average was equal to a 10 percent change in value. Today, with the benchmark stock average trading near 9,000, the same two hundred-point movement is equivalent to a less significant 2.3 percent change in price. Yet a form of the money illusion causes people to react to the nominal changes in price as opposed to the more meaningful percentage change. Fueled by a media that also falls prey to this illusion, investors often react irrationally and inappropriately, which causes a cascade of further irrational and inappropriate reactions. We'll talk more about such chain reactions later on, but the money illusion certainly plays a part in the psychology of the markets.

ODDS ARE YOU DON'T KNOW WHAT THE ODDS ARE

Steve, a thirty-year-old American, has been described by a former neighbor as follows: "Steve is very shy and withdrawn, invariably helpful, but with little real interest in people or the social world. A meek and tidy soul, he has a need for order and structure and a passion for detail." Which occupation is Steve currently more likely to have: that of a salesman or that of a librarian?

If you're like most people—at least like most of the people to whom Richard Thaler at the University of Chicago has put this question over the years—you no doubt cast your vote for Librarian Steve. And why not? Aren't librarians shy and reserved, while salesfolk are outgoing people lovers? Maybe, maybe not. But without even debating the merits of these stereotypes, there's a more fundamental reason why choosing books over sales as Steve's profession may be wrongheaded. There are more than 15 million salespeople in the United States, but only 180,000 librarians. Sure, a neighbor described Steve in a way that seems to make him unsuited for a life of sales, but one person's opinion hardly outweighs the fact that, on statistical grounds, Steve is eighty-three times more likely to be a salesman than a librarian. And while most people don't have easy access to Bureau of Labor Statistics data, the notion that salespeople far outnumber librarians is probably patently obvious to you—as is the idea that among the millions of people in sales, there are probably hundreds of thousands or more who don't match the conventional image of that profession. Given how little you really know about Steve, the fact that more people tend to be in sales than in stacks should be the major determinant in assessing the odds that Steve is a librarian.

This tendency to disregard or discount the overall odds in a given situation is what Kahneman and Tversky called "ignoring the base rate." Buying a lottery ticket can be considered something of a classic example, since the odds are overwhelmingly against your picking the right combination of six numbers. But in falling prey to Lotto fever, you are more than likely ignoring the base rate *knowingly*—few people have any confidence that they'll win. That's fine; everyone has their vices.

Even with lotteries, though, it is tough to get a good grasp of how hard the odds against you really are. For example, in a lottery in which six numbers are selected out of fifty, what are the chances that the six numbers will be 1, 2, 3, 4, 5, and 6? Most people would say that such an outcome "is never going to happen," which, although an exaggeration, does capture the long odds against such an occurrence. It is important to note, however, that the odds of 1 through 6 being selected are the same as the odds of *any* six numbers being selected. It doesn't seem right, but it is.

Another reason it can be difficult to get an accurate picture of the true probabilities is that exceptions to the overall odds are often more easily called to mind. That's why so many would-be swimmers avoided the beach after the movie *Jaws* came out in 1975.

Though fewer than seventy shark attacks had occurred in U.S. waters during the previous decade—and despite the fact that the odds against being attacked by a shark were enormous—Americans were inordinately terrified of toothy predators that summer. That's also why, after the stock market crash of 1987, many investors stopped investing in stock mutual funds for the next eighteen months or so, opting instead for cash or bonds. These folks ignored the base rate—the overwhelming historical evidence that stocks significantly outperform bonds—and focused instead on a memorable event that was more easily called to mind but highly anomalous.

Ignoring the base rate, particularly because of a misguided reliance on memorable events or on inconclusive information, contributes in a variety of ways to poor financial decisions. We say "contributes," by the way, because few financial decisions, good or bad, are the result of one and only one behavioral-economic bad habit. For example, thousands of otherwise sane amateur investors throw away good money each year in the commodities markets—you know, soybean futures and the like—because of the confluence of several behavioral-economic tendencies. These include a mistaken overconfidence in their own abilities to forecast weather on the Great Plains and a willingness to be led astray by the opinions and recommendations of others. But, knowingly or not, these investors are also guilty of ignoring the base rate. They disregard (or may be unaware of) the evidence that an estimated three out of four investors—both amateur and professional—lose money when they trade commodities.

Insurance is yet another area in which people routinely ignore the base rate and, thus, spend money needlessly. In 1995 alone Americans shelled out an estimated $8 billion in unnecessary life insurance premiums—about 10 percent of total premiums that year—on policies for which the base rate would predict that such coverage was not needed. We're talking here about flight insurance, dread disease insurance, and the like, interest in which is caused by notable but ultimately insignificant news or media events (a plane crash or a movie about the latest killer virus) that lead us to believe these calamities are more common than they are. We're not saying that the Ebola virus or cancer won't kill you or a loved one; we're simply saying that (unless there's a specific genetic reason to think otherwise) the base rate odds that it will are so long, it makes very little sense to buy a specific policy to cover the eventuality.

RAISE YOUR DEDUCTIBLE AND RAISE YOUR SAVINGS

Consumers routinely ignore the base rate when they insist on buying insurance policies—home, health, auto—with very low deductibles because they assume the chances that they will have to file a claim are greater than they actually are. Consider homeowners' insurance. A higher deductible, generally speaking, would reduce premiums on such policies by an average of 10–25 percent. But people forgo these savings because they fear having to pay a large chunk of out-of-pocket costs if they have to file a claim for property damage. What they ignore, however, is the low odds that they'll ever have to file a claim (about one in ten in any given year). Assuming the average insurance consumer raises her homeowners' policy deductible from $250 to $1,000, and assuming her annual premium falls 25 percent from $500 to $375, her total premium savings over the course of ten years would be $1,250 ($125 yearly savings times 10 years). Even if she files a claim that requires her to pay out the full deductible, her savings on average during those ten years would still be $500: $1,250 in premium savings minus the $750 difference between the $250 and $1,000 deductibles. That may or may not seem like a lot of money, but the average consumer pays $125 more in premiums each year than statistics would suggest is rational. And, of course, the benefit of a higher deductible is even greater if the money saved is invested wisely.

The final point we need to make while discussing odds is the role of chance in everyday life. Or, more specifically, the tendency to underestimate the role of chance in everyday life. As is our wont, we'll begin our lesson with a little fantasy.

Imagine you're the coach of a basketball team. There's ten seconds left in the game and your team is down by a basket. Your star player, who over the course of his five-year career has made 55 percent of his shots, is only two for ten on the night, missing several wide-open jumpshots. Another veteran player on your team has made his previous ten shots, even though his five-year career shooting percentage is just 45 percent. To whom would you give the ball for the last shot of the game?

We suspect that the majority of sports fans, and nearly everyone else as well, would probably give the ball to the player who has made ten shots in a row. Their thinking—shared by most players, coaches, and announcers—is that this player has what is often called the "hot hand." But this notion, one of the core beliefs in sports, does not hold up to scrutiny. Several years ago, Tom (along with Amos Tversky and then Stanford graduate student Robert Vallone) examined this belief by analyzing the field goal records of the Philadelphia 76ers and three other professional basketball teams. Without spending too much time on the details of their research, the inescapable conclusion from the evidence was this: Regardless of how many shots a player has made or missed in a row, the odds that he will make or miss his next shot are the same as you would expect from his overall, career-long shooting average. That is, a 55 percent career shooter is more likely to hit any given shot, regardless of his previous short-term history, than is a 45 percent shooter, regardless of his previous short-term performance. This presumes, of course, that no exceptional factors are at work—the 45 percent career shooter would have a better chance of making a layup than the 55 percent shooter would have making a much harder three-point shot.

When this research was made public—*The New York Times*'s sports page devoted a great deal of space to the matter—it was greeted with almost universal and heated opposition within the sports world. People were, and still are, unwilling to believe that the hot hand is a myth. One way to understand the myth of the hot hand is to think of a series of coin flips. The odds that a coin will come up heads on any given flip is 50 percent; there's a one in two chance. Most people know this. Yet if you flip a coin twenty times in a row—try this at home; it's safe—there is an 80 percent chance that you will get three heads or three tails in a row at some point during the series. There is also a 50 percent chance of getting four in a row and a 25 percent chance of a streak of five. But at any given point in this series, even after several heads in a row, the odds that the next flip will be heads are exactly the same as they ever were—50 percent. Similarly, what happens in basketball, and in many other sports, is that in a given series of shots there are bound to be "three or four heads in a row" or a streak of random hits or misses. Before any given shot, however, the odds that a player will make or miss the basket will roughly conform to his or her overall long-term average.

To some extent, the problems you might have in understanding the myth of the hot hand reflect the difficulty most people have with probability and statistics. Indeed, some of the greatest mathematical minds in the world can be tripped up by some of the paradoxes of probability, as was made clear earlier this decade by, of all people, Monty Hall, host of the classic television show *Let's Make a Deal.* Here's what happened: In September 1990, *Parade* magazine columnist Marilyn vos Savant—listed in the *Guinness Book of World Records* as having the world's highest IQ—published the following question from one of her readers:

Suppose you're on a game show, and you're given the choice of three doors. Behind one door is a car; behind the others, goats. You pick a door, say, number one, and the host, who knows what's behind the other doors, opens another door, say, number three, which has a goat. He then says to you, "Do you want to pick door number two?" Is it to your advantage to take the switch?

After vos Savant published her answer—saying that it's wise to switch—she was besieged by thousands of letters. These writers, whose ranks included mathematics professors from numerous universities, contended that the world's smartest person had got it all wrong. The choice between door number one and door number two, they said, was a clear case of even odds—a fifty-fifty chance that the "contestant" had picked correctly or incorrectly. Because the car is not behind door number three, they reasoned, it is equally likely to be behind door one or two. One professor remarked, "As a professional mathematician, I'm very concerned with the general public's lack of mathematical skills. Please help by confessing your error and, in the future, being more careful." Another reported, "Our math department had a good self-righteous laugh at your expense." A third suggested, "There is enough mathematical illiteracy in this country, and we don't need the world's highest IQ propagating more."

But it was they who were propagating misinformation. Vos Savant was correct. When the contestant chose door number one initially, the odds that it shielded the car were one in three—there were three doors, and behind only one of them was a car. Those odds do not change after Monty Hall reveals a goat behind door number three. After all, Monty would never open a door to reveal the car—that would ruin the drama—and at least one of the doors not chosen by the contestant is hiding a goat. Put another way, chances are that when the contestant made his or her original pick, that pick was a goat. *That fact doesn't change when there are only two doors from which to choose,* since the original choice was among three doors (two of which shielded a goat). So, assuming the contestant picked a goat (since there was a two in three chance that he in fact did), what Monty does by revealing the other goat is to let the contestant know where, in all likelihood, the car is stashed: behind door number two. Still not getting it? Don't despair. As Martin Gardner, for years the author of the mathematical games section of *Scientific American,* says: "In no other branch of mathematics is it so easy for experts to blunder as in probability theory."

Here's one more way of thinking about it. Imagine three playing cards laying facedown on the table, two black (representing the goats) and one red (the car). Now imagine that you pick one of the cards. At that moment, would you bet that you had picked a black or red card? Assuming you answered black, since the odds are two to one that you picked the darker color, you must now assume that of the two remaining cards, one is black and one is red. If you are then shown a black card (by someone who knows the color of each), the only logical conclusion, based on the probability that you picked the other black card to begin with, is that the remaining card is red. In fact, sixty-seven times out of one hundred you would be wiser to switch when offered the chance—unless, of course, you prefer goats over cars.

Whether you understand the *Let's Make a Deal* conundrum or not, it is our belief that most folks don't understand the role of chance in everyday life. Tom proves this point to his students in the following way. Every year he asks each member of his statistics class to write down a mock series of twenty random coin flips and to represent that series on a piece of paper using X's and O's for heads and tails, respectively. One student, however, is told to actually flip a coin twenty times and write down his or her results. The challenge for Tom, who leaves the classroom during this exercise, is to examine the evidence upon his return and determine which among the many pieces of paper contained the results of the real-life coin flips.

Invariably, and much to the amazement of his students, Tom always manages to identify the real-life coin flips. How? The real series of flips nearly always contains the longest streak of either heads or tails, perhaps looking something like this actual series of flips: OXXXXXOXOOXOOXOOXOOX. The *imagined* series of flips, meanwhile, often look something like this: XXOXOOOX OOXOXXOOXXOO. The students, like most everyone else, underestimate the likelihood that chance will result in long strings of heads or tails, so they don't write down any such streaks. But while it is true that in the long run the number of heads and tails will even out—as was the case in the first example cited—it is also true that there will be random instances of bunching. More important, this is also true in a variety of circumstances in life in which chance plays a surprisingly significant role.

One especially relevant example is investment performance, or more specifically the performance of mutual funds. It is true that some mutual funds outperform their peers and the market in general over time because the funds' managers have superior investment skills. But it is also true that no formula has been found to identify those brilliant managers (who are a rare breed indeed: over periods of a decade or more, roughly three-fourths of all stock funds will underperform the market). More important, it's also true that past performance, at least in the short run, cannot be counted on as an indication that the mutual fund is being run by an above average manager. The fact of the matter is that even bad fund managers will, by dint of chance, "come up heads" several years in a row—that is, they'll enjoy a prolonged series of investment successes that are just as much a function of luck as skill. In fact, University of Wisconsin finance professor Werner De Bondt estimated that more than 10 percent of stock mutual funds are likely to beat the average performance of the average equity fund three years in a row, *just as a matter of chance.*

In some parts of the country folks would explain this phenomenon by using an age-old aphorism: Even a blind squirrel finds an acorn or two once in a while. Even a lousy mutual fund manager will make a few smart investments every now and then. For investors, though, the implications should be startling. It means that even a solid record of above average performance could simply reflect a string of two or three years of especially superior results that may have been the product not of investment acumen, but of random luck. Would you bet your retirement savings on that possibility? Most people do just that. A paper published in 1996 by Columbia University business professor Noel Capon and two colleagues found that the single most common criterion people use to select mutual funds is past performance. That's true, even though many studies have shown that, at least in the world of mutual funds, past performance offers little in the way of reliable guidance about future results.

THE BIGNESS BIAS

Meet Jill and John, twenty-one-year-old twins who just graduated from college. Jill, immediately upon entering the workforce, began contributing $50 a month to a stock mutual fund and continued to do so for the next eight years, until she got married and found more pressing uses for her money. John, who married his college sweetheart immediately upon graduating and soon after started a family, didn't start investing until he was twenty-nine. Then he too contributed $50 a month to the same stock fund, and he continued doing so for thirty-seven years until he retired at age sixty-five. All told, John invested $22,200, while Jill contributed just $4,800. At age sixty-five, which of the two siblings had the most money, assuming they earned an average of 10 percent a year?

By now, no doubt, you've got the hang of the little italicized scenarios that we present to you: the seemingly obvious answer is almost always wrong. In this instance, that means Jill is the sibling who ends up with the most money upon retirement—$256,650, vs. $217,830 for John. The reason, of course, is that John could never make up for the extra eight years that Jill's money was growing while he tended to other matters. Gary has offered this problem to hundreds of people over the years, and folks usually get the answer wrong. They assume incorrectly for a number of reasons, including a failure to understand the benefits of compound earnings over time (sort of a happy mirror image of the deleterious effects of inflation over time). But we think another contributing factor is the tendency to pay more attention to big numbers and to give less weight to smaller figures. So Jill's eight years of contributions pale

against John's thirty-seven years, while John's $22,200 in annual total contributions dwarf Jill's $4,800.

If this notion—that people tend to discount the importance of small numbers—strikes you as being related to the concept of mental accounting, we couldn't be happier: you're starting to think like a behavioral economist. What makes the story of Jill and John especially meaningful, however, is that it drives home the point that failing to take small numbers seriously can have profound effects when stretched out over time. It's one thing to tack on a $500 stereo when you're buying a $12,000 new car; such things happen infrequently enough. But it's another thing to incur small expenses or small losses repeatedly over a long period; such things add up. In the world of personal finance, this mistake shows up most often and (most obviously) in the surprisingly poor performance of individual investors who trade stocks or bonds frequently: too often their gross profits are eroded by the commissions or transaction costs they incur with each trade. Though seemingly small, over time these trading costs eat away profits.

A similar phenomenon is seen in mutual funds, where the research costs, salaries, and other management expenses of a fund are represented as something called an expense ratio (fund operators are required by law to make this information public). Expense ratios from stock mutual funds range from as low as a fifth of 1 percent (of fund assets) to more than 3 percent, depending on the kinds of securities the fund buys (foreign stocks, for example, are more expensive to trade than U.S. shares) and the greediness of the fund operator. The expense ratio tells you how much the fund operator will subtract from your account every year. For example, a 1.4 percent expense ratio means the fund operator will rake off $1.40 from every $100 you have in the fund.

Given these seemingly small numbers, many if not most investors disregard a fund's expense ratio when choosing among the

thousands of options available today. Big mistake, particularly over time. Consider: At this writing, the average expense ratio for all diversified U.S. stock mutual funds was 1.41 percent. When we compare the average annual return for funds with below average expenses to funds with above average expenses, the significance of those little numbers becomes shockingly evident. Assuming you invested $10,000 in the low-cost funds, you would have $19,847 after three years, vs. the $18,805 that you would have netted had you invested in the average high-cost fund.

The 3 percent extra profit ($1,042) you would have received by investing in a fund with lower management costs is significant enough on its own, but the difference becomes even more dramatic over time, as the following table demonstrates. Had you invested $10,000 in the typical low-cost fund five years ago, you would have $24,390, a 7 percent gain over the $22,627 that you would now have if you had put your money into the average high-expense fund. And, had you been penny-wise ten years ago, your $10,000 would have grown to $35,760 today, 14 percent more than the $30,810 you would have if you had invested your ten grand in the run-of-the-mill high-expense fund. You get the idea: paying attention to small numbers can pay handsome rewards.

$10,000 invested in . . .	**After three years**	**After five years**	**After ten years**
Average-cost mutual fund	$18,805	$22,627	$30,810
Low-cost fund	$19,847	$24,390	$35,760

Based on average annual returns from 1987 through 1997.

HOW TO THINK AND WHAT TO DO

WARNING SIGNS

Number numbness may be leading you to money mistakes if . . .

- you invest in last year's hot mutual funds.
- you have very low insurance deductibles.
- you don't really understand the relationship between inflation and buying power.
- you invest without much concern about commission costs and management fees.
- you don't really understand compound interest.

There's no easy way to turn you into an expert on probability theory or a Nobel Prize–winning mathematician. There are, however, some hard-and-fast rules you can live by that will help you overcome the problems that number numbness may present.

Don't be impressed by short-term success. There are many reasons not to chase after last year's hot investment, be it a mutual fund, a variable annuity, or the stock-picking success of a particular brokerage firm. But the most important reason is that there is no earthly way of discerning if one year's performance is meaningful at all. It may simply be a matter of luck. Indeed, even a ten-year record of above average performance may reflect nothing more than one or two years of random success amid otherwise lackluster results. So when evaluating investments such as mutual funds or annuities, don't be swayed by one or two years of strong results. Even when you look at long-term performance, pay careful attention to year-by-year results. We're at least somewhat willing to believe that ten years of leading the pack is less a matter of luck than skill. But watch out: the people responsible for the ten years of success may no longer be managing the fund.

Because chance plays a far greater role than you think in investment performance, you should play the averages. You might well ask how exactly we would have you pick investments—particularly mutual funds—if you can't use past performance as a guide. This question might be particularly vexing given that we're of the belief that mutual funds are perhaps the best thing to have happened to investors and savers since banks started giving away free toasters. The advantages of pooling your money with others' to invest in a basket of diversified securities are myriad: a cheap way to spread out your risk (it would be prohibitively expensive for most investors to own shares in one hundred different companies, which is what the typical U.S. stock mutual fund owns), professional management (the folks who run funds spend all day evaluating investments), and liquidity (you can pretty much get your money any time you want).

That said, many people overestimate the chances that an individual fund manager will outperform his or her peers or the stock market in general. It's not so much that such brilliant stock pickers or bond mavens don't exist. Rather, the odds that you'll be able to identify them are small. We hope that's more obvious to you now that you understand why the performance numbers often used to promote and evaluate funds are much more the result of chance than you might have thought. Lucky for you if you manage to find an above average fund manager. If not, you would probably have been better off just investing in the stock market in general. Which, as it turns out, is exactly what we're suggesting you do, through a kind of mutual fund that's become hugely popular in recent years —index funds. Index funds are essentially mutual funds that mirror the benchmark stock averages in different categories. The archetype is the S&P 500 index fund. This sort of vehicle simply invests proportionately in the shares of the five hundred stocks that make up this average, which is generally considered the best proxy for the U.S. stock market (unlike the Dow Jones Industrial Average, which represents only the shares of thirty large U.S. companies).

The idea behind index funds is that if you can't beat 'em, join 'em. If you can't guarantee that you'll find a mutual fund manager who will outperform the average fund manager or the average stock or bond index, then it's better to guarantee that you will at least keep up with the market as a whole by investing in an index fund. Today, by the way, all manner of index funds are available. In addition to ones that mirror the general performance of large U.S. companies (as represented by the S&P 500), there are also index funds that mirror the performance of the international stock market, the U.S. bond market, the U.S. small-company stock market, and so on. Better still, because index funds don't require a lot of buying and selling—since the stocks in the indexes they attempt to mirror don't change that often—their expense ratios (and tax bills) are generally the lowest in the fund world. That's the icing on the cake—you virtually guarantee yourself better performance and more profits from the get-go because you've eliminated the high commission and management costs that other, more actively managed mutual funds can't help charging you.

Know when time is on your side and when it isn't. This is just our way of reminding you that it's too easy to overlook the deleterious effects that time, in the form of inflation, can have on buying power and to remind you that stocks have proven to be the best way to maintain buying power, given their long history of far outpacing the general rise in consumer prices. It's also a gentle reminder that it's smarter to start saving *as early as possible* for long-term goals, inasmuch as the longer your money has to earn interest and capital gains, the more you will have down the road.

This works for borrowers, too. Imagine a consumer with a $3,300 credit card balance who is being charged 18 percent annual interest and is making the minimum monthly payment. By paying a meager $10 more than the minimum each month, this fellow will pay off his debt in four years instead of nineteen years and will save almost $2,800 in interest. It works the same for mortgage payments, too: if you tacked on an extra $25 to your regular monthly payments—assuming you pay $805 a month on a $100,000 thirty-year fixed-rate loan at 9 percent—you would save $29,440 in total interest and shorten your loan by almost four years.

Stick with the base rate. Recall our earlier discussion of how people ignore base rates much too readily. There are times, certainly, when it is okay to do so—base rates represent general odds, not certainties. There are occasional warm, sunny days in Minnesota during February, but good luck trying to predict them much in advance. If unusual meteorological indicators point to a stretch of warm weather, then fine, you might go ahead and send your winter coat to the dry cleaners. In the absence of such conditions, however, it's best to keep the coat nearby. What this means is that your predictions or your bets—your investments—should follow the base rate unless you have a very good reason for them not to. This allows us to repeat the advice we've just given (pardon us, but the redundancy is worthwhile). Because of the historical superiority of stocks over alternative investment options, you should have the lion's share of your investment portfolio in the stock market unless you have a very good reason for it to be somewhere else. Also, because of the time-tested advantages of stock market index funds, you should be heavily invested in such funds unless you have a very good reason . . . You get the idea.

Read the fine print. If you invest in mutual funds, pay close attention to their fee structures, which are pretty clearly outlined in the prospectus that fund operators are bound by law to send to you before they accept your money. As a rule, you should steer clear of funds that charge more than 1 percent or so in annual expenses. A half a percentage point or more may not seem like that much of a difference, but over time it will cost you thousands of dollars. Similarly, if you invest in the shares of individual companies—something we generally discourage—remember that those transaction fees add up over time and cut into your profits. If your nest egg isn't growing as fast as your seemingly smart investing record would suggest, higher-than-expected trading costs may be one of the reasons. But only one. As you'll see in the next few chapters, you may not be as clever a stock picker as you think.

CHAPTER 5

ANCHORS AWEIGH

Which of the following guidebook descriptions for two restaurants sounds more appealing:

Restaurant one is one of the crème de la crème in the area. Dinner is served in a candlelit, romantic dining room with carved wooden ceilings, marble fireplaces, and tapestries on the wall. The menu includes veal marsala, beef tournedos, and scampi. The service is superb.

Restaurant two, according to the guide, is one of the few in the area with a national reputation. It offers all the elements for a fine dining experience. The restaurant has a tastefully appointed dining room and a menu that focuses on seafood and veal but also features some delicious beef and poultry dishes. Entrées include lobster Newburg, veal Madeira, and beef Wellington.

We have already explained how the way in which you view a decision—as a matter of selection or rejection—can have a major influence on your ultimate choice. So a person who is deciding among several stereos might choose differently if she viewed her task as deciding which *not* to buy—causing her to focus on the negative qualities of each—than she would if she viewed her mission as deciding which one to purchase, leading her to focus on the positives. Now we're set to explain a related set of behavioral-economic tendencies that can also greatly affect your decisions. Although subtly varied, these habits or inclinations share a common result: They lead people to make financial decisions based on inaccurate or incomplete information.

One is "anchoring," or the clinging to a fact or figure that should have no bearing on your judgments or decisions. The difficulties that result from anchoring, furthermore, are often compounded by a second problem known as the "confirmation bias." This bias consists of a tendency to search for, treat kindly, and be overly impressed by information that confirms your initial impressions or preferences. Coming at this from the other direction, it could also be called a "disconfirmation disinclination," because it is paired with a tendency, once you get an idea in your head, to avoid asking questions that may challenge your preconceptions. As is the case with most behavioral-economic principles, these tendencies are interesting and surprising on their own merits, with profound implications for one of the most basic and important aspects of life: the way we process and evaluate information. But they are especially important if you are to understand how you make decisions to spend, save, borrow, and invest.

NAME YOUR PREFERENCE

If the descriptions of the two restaurants at the top of this chapter sound too similar for you to choose between them, you're not alone. When Cornell marketing professor J. Edward Russo and his colleagues Margaret Meloy and Victoria Medvec offered similar profiles to a group of students, the would-be diners found no real qualitative differences between the two establishments. They pretty much said it was six of one or half a dozen of the other, which was the outcome Russo and colleagues had expected. In fact, they had carefully constructed the reviews to achieve such a measure of equality.

But a different result emerged when Russo and colleagues presented the choice to another group of students, this time with a twist. Rather than allowing these students to evaluate full descriptions of both places at once, they revealed equivalent features one pair at a time—say, restaurant one's beef tournedos with restaurant two's beef Wellington. The students were then asked to give a tentative preference as each pair of information was given. Finally, when the students had received all the relevant information for both eateries, they were asked to choose which restaurant they preferred. This time the students saw definite distinctions and had no difficulty choosing between the two places.

It doesn't matter which one each student preferred (or even whether any of them knew what beef tournedos taste like!). What matters is that they were decisive in favoring one over another, *based on whichever restaurant they had liked after hearing the first pair of attributes.* In fact, 84 percent of the students who favored the attribute of restaurant one or restaurant two in the first pairing ended up selecting that same restaurant when all the pairings were given.

So why did one set of students find little or no difference between the two restaurants while another could identify distinctions aplenty? The culprit, it seems, is the confirmation bias, or as Russo and colleagues dubbed it for their context, the "preferential bias." Whatever the name, it means that once people develop preferences —even small ones—they tend to view new information in such a way that it supports those preferences. Or, barring that, they tend to discount any new information that doesn't fit their preconceived opinions and feelings. So once a student decided that he preferred beef Wellington over beef tournedos, he felt that every attribute that came after it supported his choice of restaurant two. And any comparisons that might not have favored restaurant two probably became less important, with reasoning that might have gone something like this: "Okay, I'd prefer a romantic dining room to a tastefully appointed dining room, but I'm going there to eat, not to make love."

The psychology behind the confirmation bias results in a very common reaction to a particular type of sound decision making. People who study decision making often advise individuals who must choose between two options—say, which of two job offers to accept or which of two houses to buy—to divide a sheet of paper into four quadrants and use them to write out the pros and cons of each option. Benjamin Franklin, in fact, recommended just such a procedure. But many find the exercise unhelpful. They frequently stop midway and exclaim, "This isn't coming out right. It's not favoring the one I want!" A preference they didn't know they had suddenly asserts itself and does away with a procedure that would lead to the "wrong" decision.

The confirmation bias can affect almost any decision you make. Once you develop a feeling about an issue—no matter how unconscious that preference might be—it becomes that much harder to overcome your bias. Such a bias, by the way, can work in favor or against a particular person, product, or investment. You can get it into your head that you don't like something based on an initial reaction and subsequently be unable to view its positive attributes as significant enough to make a difference. Think about the last date you might have had, your view of a political candidate, or the first meeting with your boss. Chances are that once you developed a feeling about him or her, you viewed each new bit of information in such a way that it fit your original judgment.

The old wisdom about first impressions—that they're so important because you never get a second chance to make one—is even truer than most people realize. Once an idea sets in your head, it often sets in concrete; you can break it, but you may need a sledgehammer. In fact, we'd guess that confirmation bias might have a lot to do with the commonly held retailing wisdom that shoppers usually end up buying the first item they look at when they are out shopping. We don't know for certain if that's actually true, but if it is, there's a good chance that it's because an initial attraction to, say, a particular pair of pants results in a subsequent dismissal of other pants as you walk through the aisles. Perhaps the next pair you examine, though it has the same color, doesn't seem to have as attractive a cut. Whatever the reasoning, you find yourself unable to find another pair that matches up well enough.

All of this is fine, though, unless it distorts your decisions so that you end up spending more money than you might have if you were able to view choices objectively, from the start to the finish of your decision-making process. In fact, that your judgment can be tuned in this fashion—that you can be "programmed" to favor a product or service based on your initial impressions—is one of the basic principles of marketing and sales. It may sound obvious and simplistic, but that doesn't make it any less powerful.

Once, at a party, a friend of Gary's joined a conversation in midstream, just at the moment that one of the other guests was explaining why the high management expenses of a particular mutual fund were actually worth paying (like doctors, financial journalists find themselves in the oddest party conversations). But Gary's friend, let's call him Hank, would brook no excuse for paying such high fees. "I don't care how well the fund has done," Hank intoned. "You can find another one with lower fees that does just as well." Although Gary agreed with that statement, he also knew for a fact that Hank owned shares in another mutual fund with similarly high expenses. Gary didn't mention this point—discretion being the better part of friendship—but he couldn't help thinking that this was an example of the confirmation bias in action. Hank had invested in *his* fund based on a recommendation—from another friend—that focused on the portfolio's excellent record and renowned manager. By the time Hank got around to learning what the fund's fees were, he had discounted their significance enough to overcome any hesitations he might have had: he had developed a bias toward the fund and was subsequently unable to view new information objectively because of that bias. But at the party, when the first fact he heard about the other fund was its high fees, Hank couldn't see his way past that information. His bias was set, and everything else—*that* fund's performance record and *that* fund's respected manager—didn't seem to matter as much.

Marketers count on this very phenomenon to generate sales and brand loyalty. No matter what the product—mutual funds or mattresses, cornflakes or cars—the hope is that you'll be lured into developing a positive bias for that product and thus view subsequent information in a positive light. And, often enough, that's just what happens. For example, recent research into car buying shows how brand loyalty—a stepchild of the confirmation bias—may cost you thousands of dollars.

Here's why: Once you've developed a bias for, say, Hondas, you're more likely to view information about Hondas in a favorable light and to view any data about Nissans less favorably. One especially relevant piece of information is price, and the findings of a study by Cornell marketing professor Dick R. Wittink, along with Rahul Guah of Cornerstone Research in Cambridge, Massachusetts, suggest that people who replace cars with newer models of the same make pay more than what other consumers pay. A lot more. Analyzing data from a survey of three thousand new car buyers, for example, Wittink and Guah found that loyal Buick customers paid $1,051 more on average than customers who switched from another make to Buick. Mercedes "loyalists" paid an average of $7,410 more for their new cars than did buyers who switched to Mercedes from another make.

Although Wittink and Guah were not investigating the confirmation bias, it's hard to miss the connection. Biased toward Buick from the start, Buick owners were likely to view other aspects of that carmaker's product with less skepticism—aspects such as the dealer's asking price. On the other hand, people who weren't loyal to Buick were more likely to bargain and negotiate when they switched to that brand. This conclusion is reinforced by another finding of the study, which showed that the earlier people replaced their cars, the more likely they were to remain loyal to their make. Because repairs become more likely the longer a car is owned, those who turn in a car early are less likely to have experienced the types of problems that can challenge brand loyalty. The confirmation bias notwithstanding, it's hard to view a blown gasket in a positive light. Thus the longer people own a car, the more data they accumulate that can help to overcome the confirmation bias.

DROPPING ANCHOR

With Genghis Khan in charge, the Mongols ruled most of central Asia before their leader led them on an ill-fated campaign into what is now Hungary, where he died. Please answer the following two questions:

1. *Did these events happen before or after* A.D. *151? [Note: The number 151 was chosen arbitrarily by adding 123 to the last three digits of a New York City zip code.]*
2. *In what year did Genghis Khan die?*

Like most behavioral-economic principles—which by their very nature are woven together like strands of a tapestry—confirmation bias is both a cause and a consequence of other mental tendencies. One of them—called "anchoring"—is among the most difficult to overcome. Anchoring is really just a metaphoric term to explain the tendency we all have of latching on to an idea or fact and using it as a reference point for future decisions. Anchoring can be particularly powerful because you often have no idea that such a phenomenon is affecting you. To give you an idea of what we're talking about, let's return to our little history puzzler. Take another look at it and answer both our questions as best you can.

The first question, as you might have guessed, is nothing more than a straw man, a siren song, if you will. It's there to put a date into your head, that date being A.D. 151. Chances are that A.D. 151 did not seem quite right to you. Too early. Still, when trying to come up with a more accurate date, the 151 sticks in the mind and weighs down your estimate. The net result, in this case, is that your best guess is too low—too close to A.D. 151. (Genghis Khan actually died in A.D. 1227).

How do we know this? A few years ago Cornell's Russo put a

similar problem before five hundred MBA candidates, although Attila the Hun was the pillager *du jour* and the second question asked participants to speculate on the year he was defeated, not the year of his death. Russo asked the students to generate the first number themselves (the benchmark date in question number one) by adding four hundred to the last three digits of their own phone numbers. Interestingly, when that date happened to range between 400 and 599, the students' average guess was that Attila had been defeated in A.D. 629. But when the date they concocted was between 1200 and 1399, their average guess was A.D. 988. Although the students knew the benchmark date they had arrived at was meaningless, it still affected their guess in a meaningful way. The more recent the date, the more recent their estimated year of Attila's defeat (which actually occurred in A.D. 451).

Clever readers, of course, might ask whether the students thought the trick of adding four hundred to the last three digits of their phone number was somehow geared toward providing them with a relatively accurate benchmark date. Hard to imagine, since the last three digits of a phone number could range from 000 to 999. But more important, numerous other experiments have shown that people tend to glom on to meaningless numbers even when there can be absolutely no doubt that the numbers were irrelevant.

Amos Tversky and Daniel Kahneman, for example, asked participants in one study to estimate the percentage of African nations in the United Nations. First, a wheel of fortune—numbered 1 through 100—was spun in the presence of the experimental participants, who were subsequently asked whether their answer was higher or lower than the number that had just been spun on the wheel. Amazingly, given that the number was so obviously a matter of chance, the participants' answers were strongly influenced by the wheel's location. "For example," wrote Kahneman and Tversky, "the median estimates of the percentages of African countries in the

United Nations were 25 and 45 for groups that received 10 and 65, respectively, as starting points."

Certainly the participants in Kahneman and Tversky's experiment would have been surprised to learn that their answers were so heavily dependent on their starting point—that they unconsciously anchored on whatever number had been spun on the wheel and used it, meaningless as they knew it was, to reach a conclusion about an unrelated matter. Their surprise, though, would probably be no greater than yours if you discovered how often you anchor on some benchmark number or idea and subsequently make serious financial decisions using that as a reference point.

Have you ever been married or engaged or considered either? How much do you think a diamond engagement ring should cost? For many of you, the answer is "two months' salary." That's the "rule of thumb" most people use for answering that question, a rule promoted by the diamond industry in ad campaigns and informational material. It's a completely ridiculous figure—a ring should cost no more than you can afford! But it has become a standard point of reference for engagement ring purchases. Diamond merchants, you see, understand that by leading people to start with a dollar figure equal to two months' salary, they almost certainly guarantee more money for their industry. Why's that? Because people who might have spent less for a ring will have been programmed to think that two months' pay is the point below which they're being a cheapskate (and what man wants his fiancée to think that?). They'll anchor on the equivalent dollar figure if they don't know that this is happening—or even if they do. Meanwhile people who would likely spend more than two months' salary will do so anyway—they'll assume that the benchmark is for people who don't have as much money as they do or don't love their fiancées as much.

Note that there are really two different points here, or two types of anchoring, and both of them can be dangerous. Most people are particularly vulnerable to the effects of anchoring when they know precious little about the commodity in question. Most people, for example, have limited knowledge about how much diamonds are "really" worth and are thus that much more likely to cling to any accepted value because of their uncertainty. The anchor is not actively resisted because one doesn't know any better. But there are other times when you know the stated value is designed to mislead, but, like those respondents whose estimates were influenced by the random outcome of the wheel of fortune, you are sucked in anyway. You know the merchant in the foreign market has stated an outlandish asking price, but what's a fair amount? Chances are that the phenomenon of anchoring will lead you to adjust insufficiently from the merchant's price—even when you know you're being targeted—and thus cause you to pay too much.

If you've ever bought or sold a house, you probably know what sort of powerful drags anchors can be for buyers and sellers. Two stories illustrate this point. The first involves a woman, let's call her Molly, who was shopping for a condominium in New York City not too long ago. Molly had her eye on a perfectly nice two-bedroom condo with a view of Central Park. The seller's asking price was $1.1 million, which was in line with prices for comparable apartments at that time (this happened in New York, remember). Molly, however, had a friend who recently paid $950,000 for a similar apartment.

Because she had anchored on that figure, Molly had determined that the seller was asking too much—even though her friend's purchase had occurred before real estate prices had begun to take off. Molly loved the apartment and could afford the price, but she hemmed and hawed about it for a week, asking her agent to feel out the seller's willingness to go a bit lower. By that time another buyer appeared who quite willingly put in a bid equal to the asking price. Don't worry, though; Molly eventually got the apartment.

The bad news: She ended up paying $1.25 million, $150,000 more than she could have paid just a week before.

Such things happen in hot real estate markets, and in weak real estate markets the danger from anchoring can shift to the seller. Case in point: George and Louise, who put their house up for sale in suburban St. Louis a few years ago when George accepted a job in Dallas. Their real estate agent suggested that the couple list their house at $265,000. Although that was about $10,000 below what similar houses in the neighborhood had sold for in recent months, the agent's reasoning was that 1) the couple needed to sell quickly so they could buy a house in Dallas; and 2) their house was a little smaller than most of the homes in the neighborhood.

But George and Louise—who had paid $200,000 for the house—knew what other homes in the area were selling for, and they insisted that theirs list for $275,000. Indeed, they turned down one offer for $260,000 and a second for $265,000, convinced that their house was as good as any of the others and worth every penny of the list price. Then they waited. And waited. And waited. Unfortunately, two months after they left town—and five months after they first listed their house—a large aerospace company in St. Louis laid off several thousand workers, including many white-collar managers who lived in their neighborhood. That resulted in a flood of houses on the market, many of them bigger and in better condition than George and Louise's, which had been sitting empty for months. By the time their real estate broker finally found a buyer, seven months had passed. The final selling price: $230,000, or $35,000 less than they had been offered when they'd first listed the house.

THE POWER OF SUGGESTION

That's an awfully expensive anchor, to be sure, but before you chalk up these two anecdotes to unusual stubbornness or stupidity, remember that people can be susceptible to anchoring even when they are especially knowledgeable about the subject at hand—and therefore presumably less likely to be influenced by facts that might sway those with less experience. Consider the results of a 1987 study by the University of Arizona's Gregory B. Northcraft and Margaret A. Neale, who is now at Stanford University. Working with professional real estate agents in Tucson, the professors took one randomly selected group of brokers to a home in town and asked them to appraise its value. In addition to a guided tour, the agents received a ten-page packet of information about the house, including its $65,900 list price. Their average appraisal: $67,811. Fair enough, right? The agents applied their knowledge of the market to come up with an appraisal based on their experience (seven years, on average) and an assessment of all the relevant data.

But wait. Northcraft and Neale brought a second group of real estate pros to the house, giving them the same tour and the same packet of information, with one exception: the listing price was $83,900. This time the average appraisal came in at $75,190—$7,000 higher than the first group's. Same house, same information. The only thing that changed was the anchor—the listing price. But that was enough to change the "starting point" for these professionals and therefore dramatically influence the way they valued the house. Equally astonishing, by the way, was their complete ignorance of the power of the anchor they had received. When the agents were asked to explain their decisions, less than 25 percent mentioned the listing price as one of the factors they considered.

As we mentioned earlier, anchoring can influence almost any

financial decision you make, even when you have some expertise about the issue at hand and even when you know the anchor value was chosen to take advantage of you. That said, we can't stress enough that you are particularly prone to anchoring on a particular dollar figure when you're swimming in unfamiliar waters. The less experience you have in that ocean, the more likely it is that you'll cling to any life raft.

When you are making money decisions in areas about which you have little expertise, anchoring can trip you up on either side of a transaction. If you're on the "buy side"—purchasing life insurance, for example—you'll be susceptible to any suggestions about normal levels of coverage and premiums. All an enterprising agent need tell you is that most people your age have, say, $2 million worth of coverage which costs $4,000 a year—and that will likely become your starting point for negotiations. You might think you're being prudent (or reckless) by lowering your coverage to $1 million and shrinking your premium to $2,000 when in fact both figures may exceed the appropriate range for someone of your age and physical condition.

WHEN IS A DISCOUNT REALLY A DISCOUNT?

When Gary was working in Hong Kong a few years ago, his colleague Marge returned from a day of antique shopping with several purchases. One of them—a hundred-year-old vase—seemed expensive at a price in U.S. dollars of about $500. Marge explained that the shop owner had been asking $1,000 for the vase, but after considerable bargaining, she had persuaded him to halve the price. Marge, therefore, felt secure in the knowledge that she had bought the vase at a significant discount. This, of course, is a classic example of anchoring: Marge knew the asking price was artificial and unrealistic, but by starting the bidding at $1,000, the shop owner had anchored that figure as the reference point for the vase's value. This doesn't mean that Marge was ripped off; she was happy. It's just a reminder that a discount is only a discount if you would have paid a higher price for the item on sale. If Marge wouldn't have paid any more than $500 for the vase—or if she could have found it for less elsewhere—then the real discounting should have started at that figure.

On the "sell side," anchoring can cause you to fix on a figure—say, your original purchase price—and cling to it irrationally. This is another factor behind the phenomenon we discussed earlier, whereby people tend to hold on to losing investments longer than winning ones. If you buy a stock at $50 a share, that becomes your anchor when evaluating the worth of the stock down the road. In fact, it's not even necessary for you to have bought the stock to anchor on a price. In the early 1990s the stock of U.S. Surgical Corporation increased fourfold to $131.50 in just one year. Subsequently, when the share price dropped to $56.50 in 1992, many investors thought the stock "looked cheap" compared with its all-time high, and they rushed to invest.

They had anchored on that $131.50 and looked pretty smart for their trouble when the medical supply company's shares jumped up to $76.50. Unfortunately the stock dropped to $16 in early 1994, thanks to increased competition. Mind you, it's hard not to sympathize with those investors who anchored on the stock's all-time high. Even if the current finances or future prospects of a company in question have changed so that its shares may have justifiably dropped in value, it's difficult to erase the original purchase price (or highest price) from memory. Pulling up anchor is harder than you might think.

WHAT YOU DON'T KNOW . . .

Imagine that sitting before you are four index cards. Each has a letter printed on one side and a number on the other. The sides facing up each show one the following—A, B, 2, and 3. Your mission is to assess the validity of the following statement by turning over the fewest cards: "All cards with a vowel on one side have an even number on the other." Which cards would you turn over to determine whether that statement is true or false?

In the introduction to this book we expressed our firmly held conviction that knowledge was the key to overcoming many of the behavioral-economic obstacles we would introduce to you. By recognizing that you're prone to a way of thinking, or a pattern of behavior, you're well on your way to correcting it. While that's true, certain tendencies—particularly those discussed in this chapter—are especially hard to alter. We have already seen how people find it difficult to ignore certain anchors even when they know the value presented to them is designed specifically to mislead. You might know what a fair price is *not,* but that doesn't necessarily tell you what a fair price is or how much to adjust from that initial unfair value.

The confirmation bias we discussed earlier is also hard to overcome because most people do not find it natural to do what is necessary to overcome it—which is to deliberately seek answers that contradict their beliefs or preferences. This can be seen in the way people approach the card problem given here. Most people choose cards A and 2, or card A alone, apparently in an effort to prove the statement true. They look at a vowel card to see if there is an even number on the flip side and look at an even number card to see if there is a vowel on the other side of that. The problem, though, is that even if both cards turn out to support the rule, that's not enough. Why? Because there could be a vowel on the other side of card 3, which would mean that *not* all cards with a vowel on one side have an even number on the other. That's why the correct response would be to choose card A (to see if there is an even number on the other side) and card 3 (to make sure there's not a vowel there).

The irony, of course, is that our explanation may be hard to understand because of the very issue we're trying to explain. Because people's natural bias is to confirm what they already "know" or think they know, they reflexively try to prove a rule by looking for facts that would support it rather than looking for information that might contradict. That's why a lot of people say that ignoring card 2 is wrong, because you could flip it over and discover a consonant on the other side of card 2. But even if that turns out to be true, so what? All that proves is that a card with a consonant on one side may have an even number on the other; it doesn't prove or disprove the statement that all vowel cards have even numbers on the opposite side.

Still a little confused? Don't worry. What's important about all of this is that the failure to actively seek out disconfirming information—the only reason to pick card 3, remember, is to prove the statement was *false*—makes it that much harder to overcome the effects of preferential bias and anchoring. That's an important point to keep in mind as you try to incorporate the following advice into your financial decision-making process.

HOW TO THINK AND WHAT TO DO

WARNING SIGNS

You may be prone to the confirmation bias or anchoring if . . .

- you're especially confident about your ability to negotiate and bargain.
- you make spending and investment decisions without much research.
- you're especially loyal to certain brands for the wrong reasons.
- you find it hard to sell investments for less than you paid.
- you rely on sellers to set a price rather than assessing the value yourself.

If you think about it, the most insidious problems that stem from the confirmation bias can be summed up with a simple statement: People often hear what they want to hear. They focus on information that confirms their beliefs and explain away or disregard evidence that doesn't. As a result, many of the decisions people make are based on information that is inaccurate, incomplete, or simply inane.

In fact, Tom has discovered in his research that when people want to believe something, they scrutinize relevant information with the following question in mind—"Can I believe this?" This is a rather easy criterion to meet, since even many dubious propositions are supported by at least some evidence. When people do *not* want to believe something, in contrast, they ask themselves, *"Must* I believe this?" This is a much higher hurdle to overcome because the tiniest flaw in some body of evidence can be seized upon to condemn the proposition. It's akin to the different standards of guilt in a civil case and criminal case.

Unfortunately, knowing that such a bias exists is one thing; fixing it is another. The difficulty lies in the fact that we don't get to watch ourselves go through life from an objective point above the action: if Tom likes Gary and therefore views some obnoxious behavior on Gary's part as a lovable quirk, Tom doesn't think the confirmation bias is affecting his judgment; he thinks Gary has a lovable quirk. That's why our first piece of advice is this:

Broaden your board of advisers. We can't stress enough the importance of getting a second opinion, of conferring with other people when making large financial decisions. True, they may fall victim to the same bad habits as you. But maybe their mental bugaboos are triggered by other factors than yours, and anyway, it's a lot easier to recognize someone else's problem than your own.

When in doubt, check it out. The less knowledge you have about a subject, the more likely you are to pay attention to information that really doesn't matter when making decisions that really do—the more likely you will be to anchor on a dollar value that has little basis in reality. That's why it's important to comparison shop—not so much to find the best price as to find the correct starting point of reference. Learn to disregard meaningless information, such as the price you paid for something originally when you are selling something, or when you are a buyer, disregard what your aunt Clara's neighbor paid. Do your research and be thorough.

To set the right price when selling your house, for example, ask your real estate broker for a comparison market analysis, which will tell you the prices of recently sold homes in your neighborhood. But make sure those homes are actually comparable with yours, and be certain that the market today is comparable to conditions when those homes sold. If economic circumstances have changed, you run the risk of anchoring on a list price that might be unrealistic. If that happens, your home might languish for more than three months, the point (in a healthy market) beyond which potential buyers can start to wonder what's wrong with your place and the bids you receive might be lower than you had expected.

Home buyers, on the other hand, shouldn't be swayed by a listing price, any more than someone at an auction should be moved to value a painting at $10,000 simply because the auction house started the bidding at that level. In fact, we've always been amazed at the number of people who put in bids on homes without hiring an appraiser—or doing the necessary research themselves—to make sure the price is even remotely fair. Spending the money to get a second opinion—or, more important, a more experienced opinion—is often one of the smartest ways to overcome misleading anchor values.

Hiring a fee-only financial planner, for example, might be an alternative way to approach life insurance decisions. Such a professional—who will charge anywhere from $75 to $500 depending on the complexity of your needs—can find you the most suitable coverage for the lowest cost. Similarly, mortgage brokers or car-buying services have the expertise to evaluate prices in those respective areas without falling prey to anchoring or preferential bias. But whatever approach you choose, the greater your awareness that you might pay too much attention to facts and figures that matter too little, the greater the chance you'll avoid costly mistakes.

Get real. We could have offered this advice in any number of chapters in this book, but the idea, briefly, is that too many people have too short a memory when it comes to making financial decisions. This can lead to a bad case of anchoring. Specifically, a booming stock market and a resurgent real estate market have put a lot of unrealistic numbers in people's heads, causing a dangerous escalation of expectations. For example, incredibly high stock market returns this decade have raised the expectations of many investors (in 1995, 1996, and 1997, for the first time in history, stocks returned at least 20 percent annually three years in a row). In reality, over the long run stocks have returned about 11 percent a year, and that's hardly guaranteed in the future. So when making investment decisions, be realistic and take a longer view than you ordinarily might. An investment that returns 9 percent or 10 percent a year may seem like a dullard these days, but it's actually an exceptional opportunity.

Finally, be humble. One of the reasons people think so highly of themselves is that they often don't recognize when they've been wrong. Even when events prove a decision foolish, people frequently explain it away and emerge with their confidence intact. Stockbrokers, in fact, have a joke about this tendency, which goes something like this: "When the price goes up, the client thinks he picked a great stock. When the price drops, the client *knows* that his broker sold him a lousy one." People have an impressive knack for snatching subjective victory from the jaws of objective defeat. To be sure, faith in one's judgment—believing in your ability to make decisions that are in your best interest—is a crucial element to personal progress. But too much faith and too much confidence can lead you to unwise and unproductive decisions. As you'll read in the next chapter, overconfidence is more common than you might think.

CHAPTER 6

THE EGO TRAP

Quick! How do you pronounce the capital of Kentucky: "Loo-ee-ville" or "Loo-iss-ville"? Now, how much money would you bet that you know the correct answer to the question: $5, $50, $500?

This is probably the most challenging chapter in this book for us to write—not because the subject is complicated, but because the message we want to send might seem to fly in the face of our book's overriding premise. That premise, of course, is that individuals like you can learn from your mistakes. By identifying and understanding your behavioral-economic shortcomings, you can correct them and enjoy more financial freedom. This chapter, however, is a cautionary tale, like the yellow flag that's waved to warn race car drivers that conditions are a bit treacherous.

The core idea of this chapter is not particularly uplifting: You're probably not as smart as you think you are. That's okay; neither are we. Few people are. Indeed, for almost as long as psychologists have been exploring human nature, they have been amassing evidence that people tend to overestimate their own abilities, knowledge, and skills. In a favorable light this might be called optimism, and it's a propelling force in human achievement. It's also a bracing, cheerful way to go through life. After all, who wants to read their children a bedtime story whose main character is a train that says, "I doubt I can, I doubt I can"?

In a harsher light, though, such optimism might be called overconfidence, and in financial matters the tendency to place too much stock in what you know, or what you think you know, can cost you dearly. In fact, depending on how much you would have wagered that you knew how to pronounce the capital of Kentucky, you might already be $500 in the hole. You see, we constructed the problem at the top of this chapter to play on people's tendency toward overconfidence. Here's how: Because people are sure they know the "s" in Louisville is silent (which it is), they're confident that such knowledge is all they need to win the proffered bet. In fact, what they really need is the knowledge that the capital of Kentucky is Frankfort.

No fair? All right, we tricked you (or at least tried to). Guilty as charged. But our point is no less valid. Overconfidence is pervasive, even among people who presumably have good reason to think highly of themselves. Numerous studies over the years have demonstrated significant overconfidence in the judgments of doctors, lawyers, engineers, psychologists, and securities analysts. For example, 68 percent of lawyers involved in civil cases believe that their side will prevail, but—of course—only 50 percent can. Perhaps more important, even when people know as much as they think they know, it's often not as much as they need to know. In this chapter we will examine the pervasiveness of overconfidence, its psychological roots, and the ways it can adversely affect financial decisions. We'll also explain why it's one of the most difficult behavioral-economic traits to overcome, and we'll offer suggestions about how you might nonetheless do just that.

CONFIDENCE GAME

Give high and low estimates for the average weight of an empty Boeing 747 aircraft. Choose numbers far enough apart to be 90 percent certain that the true answer lies somewhere in between.

Now give high and low estimates for the diameter of the earth's moon in miles. Again, choose numbers far enough apart to be 90 percent certain that the true answer lies somewhere in between.

There is one other barrier we must overcome if this chapter is to be successful. Even if we can sell you on the notion that overconfidence is common and troublesome, there's a strong chance that you'll think it's not really a problem for *you.* The very tendency we're writing about could, ironically, make you overly confident that overconfidence is not one of your issues. First, overconfidence is not always arrogance. So even if you already think you're a lousy shopper, you might be worse than you think. Second, overconfidence often appears in the form of unrealistically high appraisals of one's own qualities versus those of others.

The classic example of this tendency is a 1981 survey of automobile drivers in Sweden, in which 90 percent of them described themselves as above average drivers. Clearly a large number of the respondents were giving themselves the benefit of what should have been a very large doubt. You might think you are immune to this "Lake Wobegon effect," so named after Garrison Keillor's fictional community where "all the women are strong, all the men are good-looking, and all the children are above average." But try this one: What is your usual reaction when you meet a person whom someone has said looks "just like you"? If you are like most people, your reaction is typically one of alarm, even horror: "You're kidding! Is *that* what I look like?" What this means, of course, is that the picture we carry around of ourselves in our heads is a bit more favorable than the image others have of us.

Among people who study such things, the ubiquity of overconfidence is hardly in dispute. And if you stop to think about it, signs of overconfidence are rampant in all walks of life, particularly when it comes to money. If people were not overconfident, for example, significantly fewer people would ever start a new business: most entrepreneurs know the odds of success are against them, yet they try anyway. That their optimism is misplaced—that they are overconfident—is evidenced by the fact that more than two-thirds of small businesses fail within four years of inception. Put another way, most small-business owners believe that they have what it takes to overcome the obstacles to success, but most of them are wrong.

At this juncture we should probably clarify what we mean by overconfidence. We're not talking specifically about conscious arrogance, although overconfidence might certainly manifest itself in such out-and-out hubris. It's not so much that some folks think they are especially gifted and some folks do not, although that is certainly true. Rather, what research psychologists have discovered about overconfidence is that most people—those with healthy egos and those in the basement of self-esteem—consistently overrate their abilities, knowledge, and skill, at whatever level they might place them. Over the years researchers have demonstrated the pervasiveness of this phenomenon in myriad ways. One of the more famous efforts was a series of studies in the 1970s conducted by Sarah Lichtenstein, Baruch Fischhoff, and Lawrence Phillips. Participants in these studies were first required to answer a few simple factual questions (for example, "Is Quito the capital of Ecuador?) and then to estimate the probability that their answers were correct (for instance, "I'm 60 percent sure that Quito is Ecuador's capital"). Consistently, participants overestimated the true probability; however high or low they placed the odds that their answers were correct, they were too confident with their estimates. Even for questions in which they were 100 percent certain that their answer was correct, they were right only 80 percent of the time.

You might resist the significance of these findings on the grounds that they involve only people's responses to trivia questions. "Who can get too worked up about one's knowledge of foreign capitals?" "I bet it would be different if people were asked things they care about and had more opportunities to learn." Well, in fact, researchers have done just that, by asking people questions about the one topic they care more about and know more about than anything—themselves! Psychologist Lee Ross and his Stanford colleagues Bob Vallone, Dale Griffin, and Sabrina Lin asked Stanford undergraduates at the beginning of the year whether they thought they would drop a course, join a fraternity or sorority, become homesick, and so on. On average the students expressed 84 percent confidence in their answers. But follow-up information obtained later in the year revealed that they were right only 70 percent of the time. Indeed, even when they were 100 percent certain of their predictions, their predictions were confirmed only 85 percent of the time.

A helpful way to understand overconfidence—and how it can

sneak up on you—is to take another look at the questions posed at the beginning of this section. If you haven't already, make a serious effort to choose pairs of numbers that would give you that 90 percent level of certainty. In other words, come up with answers for which you'd be comfortable betting $9 against the prospect of winning just $1 that the real answers are within your chosen ranges. Go ahead, try.

Okay, we won't keep you in suspense. An empty 747 weighs approximately 390,000 pounds, and the diameter of the moon is roughly 2,160 miles. Chances are these answers don't fall within your high and low estimates for each question. Indeed, when Cornell's Russo, along with fellow psychologist Paul J. H. Shoemaker of the University of Chicago, offered these and eight other similar questions to more than one thousand U.S. and European business executives, the majority missed four to seven of them. How is this evidence of overconfidence? Because most people who attempt to answer these questions don't recognize how little they really know about the subjects or how difficult it is to bracket high and low estimates so that there's a sufficiently strong chance that the real answer will fall somewhere in between. As a result, most people fail to spread their estimates far enough apart to account for their ignorance.

If you had said to yourself something like this—"I really have no idea how much a 747 weighs, so I better err on the side of shooting too high and too low"—then you might have spread your guesses wide enough apart. Instead what people typically do is come up with their best estimate of the plane's actual weight and the moon's actual diameter and then move up and down from those figures to arrive at their high and low estimates. Quite frankly, though, unless you work for Boeing or NASA, your initial estimates are likely to be wildly off the mark, so the adjustments up and down need to be much bolder. Sticking close to an initial, uninformed estimate reeks of overconfidence.

Yet another way to think about overconfidence and its causes is to examine what behavioral economists call the "planning fallacy." Essentially, this is the phenomenon responsible for one of the most common human foibles: the inability to complete tasks on schedule. We may not need to prove to you that such a fallacy exists, presuming as we do that your life (like ours) is filled with projects that take much longer to complete than you expected. In one interesting study, published in 1994 in the *Journal of Personality and Social Psychology,* a group of psychology students was asked to estimate as accurately as possible how long it would take to complete their honors thesis.

The study's authors—Roger Buehler of Simon Fraser University in Barnaby, British Columbia; and Dale Griffin and Michael Ross of the University of Waterloo in Ontario—also asked the students to estimate how long it would take to complete the thesis "if everything went as well as it possibly could" and "if everything went as poorly as it possibly could." Here are the results: Their best guess averaged out to 33.9 days; that's how long the typical student thought it would take him or her to finish a thesis. Assuming everything went perfectly, the average estimate for completion was 27.4 days, whereas the average estimate if things went poorly was 48.6 days. As it turns out, the average time it actually took the students to complete their thesis was a whopping 55.5 days. Depending on which estimate you use—the best, worst, or most likely case—the students were on average anywhere from 14 percent to 102 percent more confident than they should have been about the time it would take them to complete their thesis. Sound familiar?

The planning fallacy, by the way, also explains why so many public works projects take so long to complete and go so disastrously over budget. When government officials in Sydney, Australia, for example, decided in 1957 to build an opera house, they estimated that it would be completed in 1963 at a cost of $7 million. A scaled-back version finally opened in 1973 and cost $102 million. Similarly, when the city of Montreal was selected to host the 1976 Summer Olympics, the mayor announced that the entire Olympiad would cost $120 million and that the track and field events would take place in a stadium with a first-of-its-kind retractable roof. The games went off as planned, of course, but the stadium did not get its roof until 1989. And oh yes: the roof ended up costing $120 million, or almost as much as was budgeted for the entire Olympics. (Why "almost as much," even though it was the same amount? Because we didn't succumb to the money illusion that leads people to ignore the effects of inflation.)

SHOW ME THE MONEY

At this point you might be wondering how overconfidence affects financial decisions. Sure, people don't know how little they know about world capitals or plane weights—or how long it will take them to complete a college paper or to build a screened-in porch. And yes, government projects sometimes consume more tax dollars than anyone was able to forecast in advance. Folks underestimate. But what does any of this have to do with finances? As it happens, a lot. One impact is profoundly practical. Because people are overconfident, they're likely to think they are in better financial shape than they are. Consider the results of a 1996 survey of American parents by the International Association of Financial Planning. Some 83 percent of respondents with children under the age of eighteen said that they have a financial plan, while three-quarters of them expressed confidence about their long-term financial well-being. Yet less than half of respondents said they were saving for their children's education, and less than 10 percent described their financial plan as addressing basic issues such as investments budgeting, insurance, savings, wills, and estates. Is their confidence justified? Perhaps, but we doubt it.

That's one financial consequence of overconfidence: underpreparedness. Another is the willingness with which most people spend large amounts of money for products and services about which they know very little. Oftentimes, certainly, this is the result of nothing more than laziness and resignation: you realize that you know nothing about, say, washing machines, but you really don't care. You've heard of Maytag, you love those Maytag repairman commercials, so a Maytag it is. Alas, we can't help you much there. Where we can help is to point out that many people make spending decisions that they think are informed but that are in fact not very informed at all.

One of our favorite stories about this happened a little while back, when a friend Gary knows was shopping for treadmills. A few weeks earlier Gary had skimmed an article that evaluated more than a dozen brands of treadmills. Gary suggested that his friend read the article. The friend, however, thought that was unnecessary; he believed that he had learned all he needed to know about treadmills in discussions with several trainers at his health club. Gary's friend bought Brand X, Brand X fell apart three weeks after the warranty expired, Gary's friend was out $1,100. After that happened, Gary's friend went back and read the treadmill article. Sure enough, Brand X had received a subpar rating, in part because the treadmill testers found that it didn't stand up to prolonged heavy pounding. Bad news for a treadmill, really, but even worse news for Gary's friend.

Our point in telling this story is to show how a little knowledge can lead to a lot of overconfidence. Remember, Gary's friend wasn't arrogant, he didn't assume that he had some innate knowledge about treadmills. He actually spent some time researching the subject, shopping at different stores, and buttonholing the trainers at his gym. That's a lot more than many people would do in that situation. No, his problem wasn't hubris—he didn't think he was a treadmill expert—his problem was overconfidence. He thought he knew enough about treadmills to make an informed decision. He overestimated his abilities.

THE FIZZBO FALLACY

Yet another area in which overconfidence seems to thrive is residential real estate, where the acronym FSBO—or "Fizzbo" in industry jargon—stands for "For Sale By Owner." It's the term used to describe the roughly 20 percent of homeowners each year who try to sell their house without aid of a real estate agent, in the hopes of saving the 6 percent broker's commission. But Fizzbo might just as easily stand for "For Sale By Overconfident." That's because most homeowners who try to sell their house on their own underestimate the complexity of the task and overestimate their ability to handle it. Indeed, according to the nonprofit United Homeowners Association, the majority of all Fizzbos each year end up being sold through a traditional broker. More important, even those Fizzbos that are successfully completed may not be the money savers people think they are. Many times Fizzbos end up costing their owners large sums of money. It's true they save 6 percent, but because of a lack of experience the house sells for a lower price, actually costing the owner money. In other words, even though you don't have to pay a commission, you may still end up getting less than you would have had you hired a broker—perhaps as much as 10 percent less (although accurate statistics are not easily available).

There are several reasons for this. For example, some Fizzbo sellers price their home too low, and miss out on thousands of dollars of potential gain. More likely, many homeowners overestimate the value of their home—an example of the endowment effect we talked about earlier—and as a result their property takes longer to sell. The longer your home stays on the market, the more potential buyers wonder what's wrong with it and the lower the bids you'll get. A good real estate broker, moreover, has the knowledge and skills to market your home in the best possible way, and crucially, he or she is likely to generate a far greater number of interested buyers than you can, which will increase the likelihood that you'll enjoy the luxury of competing and escalating bids. This is because 85 percent of home buyers still use a broker to find homes. Finally, buyers these days know what you're up to when you try a Fizzbo: They know you're saving the broker's commission, and they will expect you to share those savings by accepting a below market bid.

UNFAIR TRADE

To be sure, none of the above necessarily means that you won't save a bundle if you sell your house on your own—or that every real estate broker is worth the commission. It's just a reminder that overconfidence can be your undoing in a variety of ways. Which brings us to the real meat of this chapter, a point that if made successfully will cause us to consider this whole enterprise a success. Our point has to do with investing, and it is bound to be seen by some as the most controversial statement in this book, the one most sure to raise eyebrows among readers. Here it is: Any individual who is not professionally occupied in the financial services industry (and even most of those who are) and who in any way attempts to actively manage an investment portfolio is probably suffering from overconfidence. That is, anyone who has confidence enough in his or her abilities and knowledge to invest in a particular stock or bond (or actively managed mutual fund or real estate investment trust or limited partnership) is most likely fooling himself.

In fact, most such people—probably you—have no business at all trying to pick investments, except perhaps as sport. Such people—again, probably you—should simply divide their money among several index mutual funds and turn off CNBC. The best that such people—yes, you—should hope for is to match the average performance of the stock and bond markets over the course of their investing life. Such a result ain't too bad.

Okay, now that we've insulted you sufficiently, let's go over our case, which at its essence is that most individual investors have no business thinking they can pick stocks or bonds with any more success than Tom and Gary would enjoy playing doubles at Wimbledon. Consider the following for a moment: As we saw earlier, the typical mutual fund manager—someone who spends every day in pursuit of brilliant investment ideas—will over the course of time be quite lucky if he or she manages simply to match the overall performance of the stock market. In fact, in most years the majority of these *professional* money managers actually performs worse than stocks in general. Indeed, over periods of a decade or more, roughly 75 percent of all stock funds underperform the market. Yes, a handful of fund managers consistently outperform the market over time, and yes, a small group of investors have

become famous over the years for exceptional stock picking. But the operative words here are "handful" and "small." The fact of the matter is that most people have no reason to think they can be more successful identifying worthy investments or timing the ups and downs of the stock and bond markets than they would be if they made their decisions by throwing darts at the financial pages.

That fact was emphasized in a 1998 study by Terrance Odean and Brad M. Barber of the University of California–Davis. Odean, you might recall, has spent a great deal of time in recent years analyzing the trading records of tens of thousands of individual investors at a large national discount brokerage firm. One of his conclusions, which we discussed earlier, was that individual investors routinely sold winning stocks and held on to losers. In his most recent work, Odean (and Barber) turned up an equally important find: that individuals who trade stocks most frequently post exceptionally poor investment results. Using account data for more than sixty thousand households, Odean and Barber analyzed the common stock investment performance of individual investors from February 1991 through December 1996. During that time, the average household earned an annualized average return of 17.7 percent—a result that itself was hardly better than the relevant benchmark index, which returned an annualized 17.1 percent during the period. More important, the 20 percent of households that traded the most—turning over roughly 10 percent of their portfolio each month, vs. 6.6 percent for all households—earned an average annual return of just 10 percent.

Think about this for a minute. It's no stretch to assume that the people who traded the most did so because they believed their stock-picking skills to be superior to those of the average investor. Yet their results were actually far inferior to those of the average investor. If that's not a sign of overconfidence, we'd be hard-pressed to explain what it might be. To quote Odean and Barber: "We

argue that the well-documented tendency for human beings to be overconfident can best explain the high trading levels and the resulting poor performance of individual investors. Our central message is that trading is hazardous to your wealth."

That's one of our central messages, too, and it further applies to those of you who have sense enough to stay away from individual stock picking but nonetheless believe you have the skill to identify those few mutual fund managers among thousands who can beat the market over time. As far as we know, there has not yet been created a reliable way to evaluate individual mutual funds with any greater degree of accuracy than there is to evaluate individual stocks or bonds. As you'll soon see, the average individual investor in mutual funds consistently fares worse than the average mutual fund, as hard as that may be to believe. Several traits contribute to this startling fact, but it is our belief that a major reason most individual investors underperform the benchmark investment averages over time is that most individual investors think they know more about investing than they actually do.

I, ME, MINE

Why is this so? Why do so many people try to time the stock market or believe they can find the next Microsoft or Home Depot? Why do so many people think so highly of their investing acumen? To some extent the phenomenon is a function of the prosperous times in which we live. At this writing, the stock market has been booming for longer than fifteen years. On Wall Street they have a phrase—"a rising tide lifts all boats"—that means that even some bad stocks go up in price when the market in general is rising. We

might just as easily coin another phrase—"a rising market lifts all egos"—that means that many people inflate the effect of their own decisions and underestimate how much of their recent investment performance is due simply to the fact that the U.S. economy and stock market have been on a roll and that they're just along for the ride. By way of analogy, if Tom and Gary had managed to sneak their way onto the roster of the Green Bay Packers in 1996, the team probably still would have won the Super Bowl that season. But that doesn't mean Tom and Gary can block or tackle or do much more to help a football team than start the "wave."

OLD DOGS, OLD TRICKS

But maybe a better question about overconfidence—financial and otherwise—is not why people are overconfident to begin with, but why they stay overconfident. You see, the problem with overconfidence is not the innate bias toward optimism that most people seem to possess. That's a good thing; it keeps the world moving forward. The problem is the inability to temper optimism as a result of prior experience. Frankly, we don't learn well enough from our mistakes. Consider: If overconfidence is as big a problem as we say it is, it should be a short-term problem at worst. The learning process would ideally go something like this: We think highly of ourselves, the world and events show us who is boss, and we become less confident and more realistic about our knowledge and skills. Yet in the main, this doesn't happen. In their analysis of the planning fallacy, Buehler, Griffin, and Ross discussed several reasons people consistently fall prey to that type of optimism and overconfidence. One reason was a persistent habit of focusing on future plans rather than past experiences. We can always envision specific reasons why *this* project will get done on time. But the best laid plans are typically done in by elements we cannot anticipate. What a focus on the specifics of a particular project does, then, is force us into an "inside" view of the problem that distracts us from thinking about how infrequently we get things done as quickly as we initially expected. In our experiences, a similar phenomenon happens to investors, the result of this and several habits that we suspect you'll find very familiar.

HEADS I WIN, TAILS IT'S CHANCE

The average reader might have a ready explanation for the dogged persistence of overconfidence, an explanation that goes something like this: "People stay overconfident because they conveniently remember their successes but repress or forget their failures." That's not far off: there are psychological forces at work that can indeed make our triumphs more memorable than our defeats. But as is so often the case in psychology, the true story is a bit more complicated. Sometimes our *failures* are the most vivid memories of all. If you were ever one word away from winning a spelling contest, for example, it's a lock that you'll carry the memory of the word that eliminated you to the grave.

But here's how overconfidence is preserved: Even when you remember your defeats, you may remember them in a way that alters their perceived implications for the future. Harvard psychologist Eileen Langer describes this phenomenon as "heads I win, tails it's chance." The idea here is that when things happen that confirm the correctness of your actions or beliefs, you attribute the events to your own high ability. Conversely, when things happen that prove your actions or beliefs to have been mistaken or wrong-headed, you attribute those disconfirming events to some other cause over which you had no control. The net result is that you emerge from a checkered history of success and failure with a robust optimism about your prospects for the future. A little better luck, or a little fine tuning, and the outcome will be much better the next time.

Case in point: A fellow Gary knows invested in Applied Materials in 1996 because the company was the dominant supplier of the machines that computer makers use to make their chips. And he took full credit when the stock raged over the next year. He proudly explained that he understood better than most how ubiquitous computer chips were becoming and how changing technology required manufacturers to constantly update their equipment. His confidence in his ability to pick winners soared. On the other hand, when economic problems in Asia pulverized the share prices of all semiconductor equipment makers in 1997, his confidence in his investing acumen was not shaken. After all, how could he know that Asia's woes would hurt Applied Materials' profits? Well, one answer is that he might have known had he bothered to learn that 50 percent of semiconductor equipment purchases at the time originated in Asia. The better answer is that Gary's friend, who is not in the semiconductor business, might not be the best person to evaluate the future of the companies that manufacture chip-making equipment.

But what if Gary's friend worked in the computer industry? What if he did understand the vagaries of the chip-making cycle? Wouldn't that qualify him to invest in high-tech companies? Before you answer, take a look at the next section.

ALL TOO FAMILIAR

The last contributor to investor overconfidence that we want to mention is a hybrid of sorts. In many ways it's a variation of the endowment effect we explained earlier, whereby people tend to place an inordinately high value on what is theirs, relative to the value they would otherwise place on such things. But this principle applies not only to concrete items, but to ideas as well. Essentially, we place too much value on what we know from our own personal experience simply because it is from our own personal experience. To illustrate, we'll turn to a 1997 study by Gur Huberman, a finance professor at Columbia University in New York City. Huberman was intrigued by the fact that throughout the world, most investors own more stock of companies in their own country than of those in foreign countries.

To some extent, certainly, this reflects the ease of investing domestically; you don't have to worry about another country's laws or currency exchange rates. But Huberman thought that another factor might be at work, a psychological need on the part of investors to feel comfortable about their investments, with that comfort coming from familiarity. This may seem perfectly reasonable, but it may also be another example of overconfidence, inasmuch as investors might overestimate their knowledge about companies and stocks simply because they are more familiar with them.

To test his theory, Huberman examined the stock ownership records of (what were then) seven U.S. "Baby Bells," the regional phone companies created by the government breakup of AT&T in the 1980s. His research showed that in all but one state (Montana), more people held more shares of their local phone companies than any other Baby Bell. Again, this may make perfect sense to you: if a person thought regional phone companies were a good investment, why not invest in the one with which they are most familiar? Well, one reason might be that their phone company wasn't the best of the seven Baby Bells. On average, in fact, the odds were six to one against. And since we're pretty sure that most of the investors in question didn't conduct research that showed their Baby Bell to be superior, the only conclusion to be reached is that investors had a "good feeling" about their phone company relative to the others simply because it was their phone company.

This idea—invest in what you know—has become increasingly popular in recent years, associated with such investing legends as Peter Lynch, manager of the highly successful Fidelity Magellan mutual fund for thirteen years, and Warren Buffett, longtime chairman of the even more successful Berkshire Hathaway holding company. Indeed, it is often recounted how Lynch loved the coffee at Dunkin' Donuts and made a fortune investing in the company's stock or how Buffett's addiction to Cherry Coke was a key component in his decision to invest in Coca-Cola shares before the company's stock exploded.

Similarly, the "invest in what you know" approach is at least partly responsible for the fact that employees typically allocate more than a third of their retirement account assets to the stock of the company for which they work, despite the risks of such a strategy: your biggest investment—your job—is already tied to the fortunes of your workplace, so by stashing retirement assets in your company stock, you're putting too many eggs in one basket. That's why most financial planning pros recommend you keep no more than 10 percent of your 401(k) assets in your own company's shares.

In any event, the problem with all of this is that people overconfidently confuse familiarity with knowledge. For every example of a person who made money on an investment because she used a company's product or understood its strategy, we can give you five instances where such knowledge was insufficient to justify the investment. A classic example is Apple Computer. Without debating the merits of the PC versus the Macintosh, it's safe to say that many Mac users were convinced the company's technology was superior to that of its competitors, and as a result, many of them invested in Apple's shares with exceeding confidence. What these investors couldn't foresee was that Apple's strategy to forgo licensing its technology to clone makers would leave the door wide open for PC manufacturers to pounce. As a result, the only thing that seems to have shrunk faster than Apple's share of the personal computer market is its stock price. Because this entire book was written on Macintosh machines, we're hoping that Apple makes a comeback, but so much for investing in what you know.

HOW TO THINK AND WHAT TO DO

WARNING SIGNS

Overconfidence may cost you money if . . .

- you make large spending decisions without much research.
- you take heart from winning investments but "explain away" poor ones.
- you think you are "beating the market" consistently.
- you make frequent trades, especially with a discount or on-line brokerage.
- you think selling your home without a broker is smart and easy.
- you don't know the rate of return on your investments.
- you believe that investing in what you know is a guarantee of success.

Although you might not have guessed it, it was not our goal in this chapter to beat all remnants of self-confidence out of your system. Some of you may be every bit as smart as you think you are, and far be it from us to keep the next Peter Lynch or Warren Buffett from making his or her mark on the investment world. Our goal, rather, was twofold. First, we'd like to convince most of you to cast the bulk of your investment lot with the overall market by investing almost exclusively in index mutual funds. Because we make the case for this approach elsewhere in the book, we won't belabor the point here. But the plain truth is that most investors miss out on potential profits because they believe they can outthink the market when all evidence says they can't.

Our second goal is based to some extent on the belief that we won't easily achieve our first. Most of you will continue to pick individual stocks, bonds, funds, and the like in part because you think you have the skill and in part because it's fun. That's okay—it is fun. What we hope to have accomplished in this chapter is to convince you that you are likely overestimating your abilities and thus need to reevaluate the effort you put into investment decisions (and spending decisions, too). We don't want to abuse you, just humble you, so that you'll be less likely to make mistakes that cause you to lose money or miss out on gains.

Investor, know thyself. Maybe you *are* as good an investor as you think. But experience tells us that many people overestimate their hit-to-miss ratio, either because they conveniently ignore or explain away their failures or because they don't do a full accounting when calculating their performance records. In other words, your market-beating 15 percent average annual gains might really be a solid 10 percent or an anemic 5 percent if you count the commissions you paid and the taxes you incurred. This is especially true for active traders who buy and sell stocks on a daily, weekly, or monthly basis.

We're against such an approach, but if that's your passion, it is essential that you review your investment records carefully, keeping these costs in mind. Because the math required for this effort can often be quite complicated, we suggest you avail yourself of any number of fine computer software programs oriented toward investment record keeping. Or you might simply go to the bookstore and pick up any number of investment books that offer worksheets to figure this out. Be warned, though: What you discover may be a blow to your ego.

If you are a person who's prone to kicking yourself for investment opportunities that you missed, we suggest you undertake the following exercise. For at least a month, write down every investment idea that you have, then tuck that paper away in a drawer somewhere. In about a year take it out and see how all your picks have done. We suspect that while several will have outperformed the market, an equal or greater number won't. Again, this is a useful and interesting way to avoid succumbing to fond memories.

Take 25 percent off the top (and add 25 percent to the bottom). Unfortunately there's no hard and fast rule for quantifying how big a problem overconfidence and optimism may be for you or anyone else. Nonetheless, a helpful way to deal with overconfidence is to incorporate an "overconfidence discount" into your projections, both on the upside and on the downside. This notion, as it happens, is already a common rule of thumb in some areas of life. For example, most experts counsel homeowners to add 10 percent to contractors' remodeling estimates, in terms of both cost and completion time. Our experience suggests 25 percent may be a better figure, but you can choose whatever number you're comfortable with. The key is to apply the discount on both sides of the transaction. For example, if you're thinking about investing in a stock, force yourself to come up with a realistic performance appraisal over your intended holding period, as well as the potential downside if things go wrong for the company. Then subtract 25 percent from your optimistic forecast and add 25 percent to your doomsday scenario. If the trade-off between potential risk and reward still seems worth it, go ahead. If not, you might want to walk away. In either case, though, the exercise is almost certain to make you consider aspects of the investment that you had otherwise ignored or forgotten.

Get a second opinion. This advice, about as commonsensical as we can get, is a great tonic for people who tend to think too highly of their own experiences. But what we're suggesting may not be what you're thinking. Yes, it's always a fine idea to ask your friends and other knowledgeable people what they think about an investment or purchase you're considering. But what if they are as overconfident or uninformed as you are? For example, what good did it do for Gary's friend to have asked his trainer about treadmills? Our idea is slightly different. We're suggesting that when you make important financial decisions you should ask trusted friends or experts what they think of your decision-making *process.* In other words, don't ask if they agree with your decision, ask if they think the way you went about reaching your decision was wise and thorough. Had Gary's friend asked him that question, Gary might have said that he thought it unwise to ignore the opinions of the professionals at the ratings magazine whose job it is to evaluate products.

But even as we recommend you seek counsel from others, we must once again throw up a yellow flag of caution. As you'll learn in the next chapter, people often rely *too* heavily on the opinions and actions of others. You may not be as smart as you think you are, but you may still be smarter than many other folks.

CHAPTER 7

I HERD IT THROUGH THE GRAPEVINE

George and Jane recently bought a new Chrysler Town and Country minivan for $28,000, after carefully researching their decision. Oddly, over the next few months a flood of strangers began offering the couple smaller and smaller amounts of money to buy it from them. As far as they could tell the vehicle was in fine shape; a few thousand miles and a ding or two, but otherwise the engine was purring. Still, George and Jane seriously considered selling the Chrysler for half what they paid because they worried something might have been wrong. Should they have sold?

Before you snicker at the silliness of the above question—"Why on earth should they sell their van simply because people keep offering them less and less for it?"—ask yourself what your advice to George and Jane might be if it wasn't a Chrysler minivan they were considering they should dump, but one thousand shares of Chrysler stock they had purchased for $28 a share and that had recently fallen to $14. We're pretty sure that many of you would advise the couple to sell their Chrysler shares in a hurry. In fact, we're certain of it, since several hundred years of stock market history have shown that all too often that's what many investors do: they buy stock in companies or shares in mutual funds, presumably for sound reasons, but often sell those shares the minute "the market" turns against them. They cut and run as soon as a bunch of complete strangers start offering them less and less for their investment than what they paid. Conversely, many investors will pay higher and higher prices for stocks (or paintings or real estate or almost anything else) simply because other people they don't even know are willing to pay such prices.

On Wall Street they call this "investing with the herd," and the pervasiveness of this approach to managing money is expressed in another securities industry aphorism, "The trend is your friend." In other words, don't outthink the road signs. If the bulk of investors think Consolidated Cornbread is a wonderful stock, who am I to disagree? If they decide next month that widgets are a thing of the past, well, they must know what they're talking about. Even people who exhibit the sort of overconfidence we discussed in the previous chapter can fall victim to this lemminglike behavior. That's because their overconfidence allows them to overestimate their ability to identify what "the smart money" thinks about a particular investment or company and to make investment decisions accordingly.

Of course, the notion that people tend to conform to the behavior of others is among the most accepted principles of psychology.

It should also be patently obvious to even the least introspective person. No matter what you call it—peer pressure, conforming to the norm, or "going along to get along"—your life is filled with instances large and small in which the thoughts or actions of a larger group or community influence your individual decisions. Have you ever seen a film simply because "everyone else" seems to be seeing it? Or bought a best-seller for no better reason than because it's a best-seller? Sure you have. Mostly such conformity is a good thing, and it's one reason societies can function: if people in general didn't accept standards of behavior, it would be impossible to drive a car without fear of head-on collisions, let alone hope to establish a system of law and government in which people by and large agree to follow a specific ideology (say, democracy) and a body of rules.

So we're all for conformity in many of its guises. The problem arises when people conform to larger habits or trends that may go against their own interests. In financial terms that means allowing the judgment of others to steer you into unwise investments, or out of sound ones. You see, our concern is with the manner in which value is determined—or, more precisely, the manner in which you allow other people to determine the value of things for you. To some extent, certainly, what other people think matters a great deal. Beauty may be in the eye of the beholder, but value is often in the eye of the buyer. We might think this book is worth $250 a copy—but if readers don't agree, we're out of luck. Similarly, if George and Jane had *wanted* to sell their minivan, then it was truly worth only what people were willing to pay for it—but only if George and Jane wanted to sell. If they didn't, then the value of their Chrysler was theirs alone to decide. What happens too often, though, is that the Georges and Janes of the world let outside forces tell them when

it's time to sell and to buy. They allow popular opinion and behavior to define value for them—sometimes for the good, but often not.

In this chapter we're going to explore the way herds get rounded up and the ways that people are surprisingly prone to joining them. We're going to focus on investing, because it's the most obvious way to explore the phenomenon, but the principles can apply to almost any financial decision in which you tend to follow the leader. It's a complicated issue, because typically the opinions of others—a friend, a financial adviser, a loved one, or the general public—should count for something. That's why understanding when to go along and when to buck the trend can have a sizable impact on your finances. As you will see, people who rely on the madding crowd for investment advice often end up the poorer for their trouble.

WORSE THAN AVERAGE

Fact #1: From 1984 through 1995 the average stock mutual fund posted a yearly return of 12.3 percent, while the average bond mutual fund returned 9.7 percent a year.

Fact #2: From 1984 through 1995 the average investor in a stock mutual fund earned 6.3 percent, while the average investor in a bond mutual fund earned 8 percent.

Question: What's wrong with this picture?

The two statements you just read, both of which are true, should strike you as extraordinarily strange—the equivalent of being told that the average commercial jetliner flies at an altitude of thirty-five thousand feet, while the average passenger in a commercial jetliner flies at fifteen thousand feet. How can this be? How can mutual funds, generally described as the best thing to happen in personal finance since dividends were invented, often be such a disappointing deal for their investors? How can funds earn more than the people who own them? Here's how: Rather than investing in a few well-researched mutual (ideally index) funds and holding on to them for a very long time through thick and thin—the classic "buy and hold" strategy—most people flit in and out of a whole passel of funds in an effort to maximize their returns.

That tendency has become ever more common in recent years, as the number of mutual funds has exploded and the information about them has increased in availability. Today the typical fund shareholder—there are about 40 million of them in the United States alone—hangs on to a fund for less than seven years, compared with an average holding period of more than sixteen years in 1970. And that's only an average: millions of investors find that bouncing in and out of funds is as easy as dialing a toll-free telephone number—which, of course, it is.

None of this would matter, though, if folks managed to switch into funds that performed better than the ones they leave behind. The problem is that they don't, and much of the reason can be attributed to the folly of herd investing. That's because fund hoppers are generally playing a financial version of follow the leader. Unhappy with the lagging performance of their current investments, they pour their cash into other funds that have posted strong recent returns or whose assets have been growing by leaps and bounds thanks to a rush of other investors. Typically these funds have recently received favorable recommendations from a research service such as Morningstar or from any number of personal finance publications or programs.

The trouble is, when you chase after strong past performance the trend is very often *not* your friend, for two reasons. First, a fund's record often looks best just before its investment strategy stops working (remember the phenomenon of regression to the mean that we discussed in the introduction?). Consider, for example, the gangbuster performance of mutual funds that invested in shares of companies in the fast-growing Pacific Rim. Had you jumped on that bandwagon in early 1997—as many investors did—you would have received quite a jolt when economic turmoil sent the stock markets in that region spiraling earthward. That leads us to our second point: Unless you're among the first in line, chances are you're investing at a time when the prices of the stocks or bonds in which your new fund invests have already enjoyed a steep climb. So you're investing with the herd, only you're at the end of the pack. The result: Many investors take their money out of poor-performing funds just before they begin to rebound and put their dough into zooming funds just before they stall. Then they repeat the cycle all over again.

Are we contradicting what we said earlier when we urged readers not to sell their winners too quickly and hang on to their losers too long? Not at all. The "average" winner is unlikely to be the type of "flavor of the month" investment we are discussing here—one that has been run up excessively and is thus headed for a steep fall. Thus an investment that has been doing well during the time you've owned it shouldn't be sold simply because you're nervous about not locking in the profit you've made. If it's a sound investment, there should be more gains on the way. Note that the information you receive about such investments (the sound performance and solid investor confidence that is reflected in the rising price) is quite different from the type of information you receive about the latest "hot" investment (the frenzied interest you've heard about second-hand). It is hardly a contradiction to say that you should be more swayed by the former than the latter.

More than anything, it's this "sell low, buy high" approach that keeps shareholder returns below that of the funds in which they invest. Consider this example, courtesy of *Money* mutual fund columnist Jason Zweig. In 1997 Zweig—along with *Money* reporter Malcolm Fitch and former Securities and Exchange Commission economist Charles Trzcinka—analyzed the total returns reported by more than one thousand U.S. stock funds for 1996 and more than eight hundred funds for the three years that ended in December of that year. Among their findings, the average shareholder at more than a dozen *profitable* U.S. stock funds actually *lost* money in 1996. And many more investors, who weren't quite so unlucky as to lose money while their fund was profiting, nonetheless fared far worse than they might have expected.

Zweig illustrated his point with the case of PBHG Core Growth, an aggressive stock fund that had more than $50 million in assets at the beginning of 1996. In the first three months of the prior year, while the benchmark S&P 500 index of stocks rose 5.4 percent, PBHG Core Growth zoomed an even more impressive 18.2 percent. Indeed, for the entire year the fund returned a whopping 32.8 percent, compared with better than 28 percent for the S&P 500. The problem, though, was that most people who invested in PBHG Core Growth that year missed most of the good stuff. Here's the math: At the end of March the fund had just $31 million in assets. But after its eye-popping performance in the first quarter—duly noted in the press and in the fund's ads—a pack of fund hoppers pounced into the fund: in May and June they added more than $200 million to PBHG Core Growth's assets. Too bad, since in the second half of the year the fund lost 3.8 percent. So even though the fund gained more than 32 percent over the year, its average shareholder *lost* 3 percent.

RUNNING WITH THE BULLS

Mutual funds are hardly the most obvious example of herd investing. It's a far more common phenomenon within the context of individual securities, particularly stocks. In fact, we could offer dozens, indeed hundreds, of examples in which investors follow the unspoken "advice" of their peers and rush to buy shares of one or another rising star. Instead we'll mention just one, involving a Calgary, Alberta, gold-mining company called Bre-X. In 1996 and 1997 officials of this little-known Canadian outfit began touting a major gold discovery at Busang, a jungle site on the Indonesian island of Borneo. Not surprisingly, the stock shot up from a couple of bucks in 1995 to $19.50 in September 1996. Now, there's always a chance that this was not a case of herd investing—that, instead, thousands of individual investors understood the complicated vagaries of the gold-mining business and determined that Bre-X's claims were legitimate (they weren't). We doubt it, though. More likely, as some investors began to bid up the company's stock price, even more investors decided that they didn't want to miss out on all the fun and capital gains. No matter that many of Bre-X's top officials were selling their shares at these inflated prices or that the company hadn't started producing gold from its new El Dorado. In fact, many investors probably didn't know or care that much about future gold production. Their aim, no doubt, was to sell their Bre-X shares to other investors for more than they had paid, hopefully a lot more—just like the folks from whom they had bought their shares. Like many instances of herd investing, Bre-X was a pyramid scheme of sorts: the earlier you get in on such run-ups, the better off you are. On the other hand, if you're unlucky enough to be late in the chain, the penalty for tardiness can be costly. In early 1997 independent tests revealed that Bre-X's claims were unfounded, and management was eventually suspected of a massive stock fraud scheme. At this writing, the company's stock is worthless.

It may seem to you that we're just stating the obvious. Even the most inexperienced investor knows that money can be lost by running headlong with the bulls into a dubious investment. But not as many people remember that herds move both ways, causing many people to abandon perfectly fine investments. One illustrative example of herd investing that resulted in a missed opportunity had its start soon after President Clinton was elected and began his much ballyhooed efforts to reform the nation's health care system. Given the size of the task—the health care industry in all its incarnations accounted for roughly one-seventh of the U.S. economy at the time—and the difficulty of even conceiving an appropriate way to implement change, investors were understandably concerned about the future of health care companies.

This concern tended to manifest itself as pessimism—understandably so, when you consider that the implied goal was to cut the rising levels of health care costs. That could only hurt the profits of health care providers, especially pharmaceutical makers, whose impressive stock price growth over the previous decade was fueled by the firms' immense drug profits. That's what the "smart money" said, and that's what drove down prices of all health care companies, including such blue-chip companies as pharmaceutical giant Johnson & Johnson. Indeed, professional stock pickers began selling their J&J shares in early 1992, followed quickly by a horde of individual investors. One woman explained her reasons for dumping her J&J shares in early 1993 and pretty much summed up the general feeling of her investing peers: "I don't know how health care reform is going to turn out, but if Washington gets involved, it's not going to be good." As a result of such widespread sentiment, J&J's share price plummeted from $59 to $36 over an eighteen-month period.

But there was one flaw with the market's reasoning, and it wasn't even that health care reform never materialized. It was the fact that if investors had been paying attention to Johnson & Johnson's actual business fundamentals, they would have noticed that 1) J&J manufactures lots of other things besides drugs, such as baby shampoo, contact lenses, and Band-Aid adhesive strips; and 2) the company's profits were continuing to rise even as health care costs in general were stagnating. Instead, too many investors paid heed to what other investors thought of the company's prospects under health care reform. The cost? After bottoming out at $36, J&J's stock almost doubled to $65 by the end of 1997.

THE MADDING CROWD

Using the Bre-X and Johnson & Johnson anecdotes as examples of herd investing gone wrong is a bit like shooting fish in a barrel. They're so extreme as to be parodies of the genre. But we dredge them up for a reason different from the ease with which both confirm our thesis. Despite their disparate corporate profiles—J&J is one of the best-known companies in the world, while Bre-X was a shell that enjoyed a brief moment in the spotlight—the fortunes of both organizations and their industries were chronicled extensively in the media during the periods in which we examined their investment performance. This fact is extremely important if you are to understand how investing trends start and how you might avoid falling victim to them. But first a little background.

Through the years, a variety of social mechanisms have been identified as the major causes of (or catalysts for) uniformity of behavior—that is, there are a variety of different ways that people learn to conform to the actions of others, learn to *want* to conform, and learn to decipher the clues that dictate how that conformity should manifest. One such mechanism might be called "sanctions": children learn that temper tantrums are frowned upon when they are sent for a "time-out." Adults learn that assault is unacceptable when they are arrested for it, and they learn that removing money from a tax-deferred retirement account is a no-no when they are levied with a 10 percent early-withdrawal penalty. The flip side of sanctions is positive reinforcement: behaving in class brings praise from teachers, just as keeping your lawn manicured earns the approval of neighbors. Such enforcement can be obvious (the government encourages people to save for retirement by offering tax breaks) or implied (some people seem to think you're "hip" when you wear the latest fashions, so you keep wearing them).

Whatever the mechanism, though, the desire or tendency to conform—to follow in the footsteps of others—is enhanced when people are in a state of uncertainty or confusion. If you throw an otherwise self-confident corporate chieftain into unfamiliar territory—say, a climbing expedition up Mount Everest—she is probably more likely to do as the Sherpas do than as she would in the executive dining room. Any alternative looks appealing in a vacuum: when you don't have any idea what to do or how to behave —particularly in times of crisis or anxiety—the fact that a lot of other people seem to have a plan is a very compelling reason for mimicking them.

That's especially relevant in any discussion of money and investing. As an increasing number of people become involved in the stock market—say, by dint of retirement plans at work—they are often thrown into situations about which they know very little and about which they are subjected to various and competing sorts of advice. Doing what everyone else does is not an unreasonable alternative in that situation, and it has a bonus allure: If your decision turns out to be unwise, you can at least comfort yourself with the knowledge that a lot of other people made the same decision (some of whom may even be famous). It's not so much that misery loves company as that misery loves to avoid blame.

In any event, the more uncertain people are—and the higher the stakes involved—the more vulnerable they are to the sort of cue taking that leads to herd behavior. That's why teenagers are presumably more likely to succumb to peer pressure than adults. They have less experience to draw upon when evaluating the pros and cons of conforming, and the stakes are higher: going one's own way really does have greater consequences for a seventeen-year-old than for a thirty-seven-year-old. But the stakes are pretty high even for adults when the issue is money, a fact that often leaves investors in a highly vulnerable state of mind: they're desperate for guidance, ripe for taking cues from almost anyone.

This heightened sensitivity to the actions of others dovetails nicely with a recent theory about fads, trends, and crowd behavior. In a 1992 paper in the *Journal of Political Economy,* the University of California–Los Angeles' Sushil Bikhchandani, David Hirshleifer, and Ivo Welch described a phenomenon they called an "information cascade." Their work sheds light on one of the great puzzles of finance and economics: Why do investors consistently "overreact," paying too much for securities that later fall in price (and too little for investments that turn out to be worth far more)?

Essentially, their theory posits that large trends or fads begin when individuals decide to ignore their private information and focus instead on the actions of others, even if that action conflicts with their own knowledge or instincts. Think about a traffic jam on a freeway and how you might be tempted to follow a driver who abruptly veers onto a little-used exit, even if you doubt that it will save you any time. The actions of a few people lead others to mimic their behavior, which in turn leads even more people to imitate that behavior, and so on. What's especially interesting about their theory is that it showed that even the smallest bit of new information can lead to rapid and wholesale changes in behavior. As they wrote: "If even a little new information arrives, suggesting that a different course of action is optimal, or if people even suspect that underlying circumstances have changed (whether or not they really have), the social equilibrium may radically shift." In other words, it doesn't take much for the terrain to shift dramatically.

This observation rings especially true in financial markets, where new information arrives by the second. That's why the Johnson & Johnson and Bre-X anecdotes are so illustrative. Both situations were heavily monitored by the news media, which offered regular bits of new information (some important, some not) that caused those who follow the minute-by-minute movements of stock prices to take action. Their action subsequently led to even more investors following suit. This only reinforced the apparent wisdom of the initial investors, leading them to repeat their actions.

Think about it this way: You sell (or buy) a stock, which causes its share price to fall (or rise). This leads other investors to sell (or buy) their shares, which causes the price to fall (or rise) even more, which leads you to repeat your actions. That's how a stock market crash—and, in the opposite direction, a stock market bubble—gets started. But what's even more important to understand about all of this—not just in the case of J&J and Bre-X, but with respect to all securities—is that very often the forces that move markets and investment prices, at least in the short run, are not directly related to the true worth of the underlying assets or companies. Powerful information cascades lead people to sell simply because other people are selling, or to buy because other people are buying.

NO NEWS IS GOOD NEWS

There's a good reason for you to pay less attention to financial news, print and electronic: Investors who tune in too closely to financial reports probably fare worse than those who tune the news out. We really can be trusted on this one: After all, for fourteen years Gary made his living providing just this sort of news. Paul B. Andreassen, then a psychologist at Harvard, demonstrated this by comparing the performance of four groups of mock investors. Using the stock prices of real companies and real news reports, two of the groups made simulated investment decisions about a relatively stable stock—its share price didn't vary much over the course of the experiment. However, one group was subjected to constant news reports about the company, while the other received no news. A similar test was given to two other groups, although the stock in question was subject to wider price swings than the shares of the other company. The results: Investors who received no news performed better than those who received a constant stream of information, good and bad. In fact, among investors who were trading the more volatile stock, those who remained in the dark earned more than *twice as much money* as those whose trades were influenced by the media.

Remember that one of the basic principles of modern economics is that the market is efficient. That is, stock prices reflect all the knowledge and experience of investors, so it's useless to try to pick stocks because the market knows better than you. You'd do just as well throwing darts at the stock listings of the newspaper.

This may or may not be true over time. But numerous studies have shown that, in the short run at least, investors are notoriously off the mark when assessing the worth of companies on a day-to-day, or even a year-to-year, basis. Partly because of information cascades—because people are prone to go with the flow—investors frequently overreact to both good and bad news, causing the prices of favored companies to rise too high and prices of tainted companies to fall too low. A good example of this phenomenon turns up in a study published in the *Journal of Finance* in 1985, authored by the University of Chicago's Richard Thaler and Werner De Bondt of the University of Wisconsin.

Thaler and De Bondt, widely known for their exploration of securities' price movements, analyzed the performance of stocks listed on the New York Stock Exchange (NYSE) that had either risen or fallen in excess of the average ups and downs of share prices in general. They examined six-year and ten-year blocks of time, which they divided in half. Then, using returns from the first half of each period—what they called the "formation period"—they came up with separate portfolios of winners (stocks whose gains were above average) and losers (shares whose drops were steeper than average). Finally, they examined how the winners and losers performed over the second half of the study periods (the "holding period," in their words). Their findings: "Extreme returns of stocks listed on the New York Stock Exchange were found to be subsequently followed by significant price movement in the opposite direction. Using ten-year blocks of time, loser portfolios earned from the beginning to the end of the five-year holding periods an average of 30% more than the winner portfolios. Using the same procedure with six-year blocks of time, losers outperformed winners by almost 25% during the three-year holding periods."

Let's restate that in simpler terms. Thaler and De Bondt showed that when investors react in extremes—remember, they looked at stocks whose prices bounced up or down in excess of the movements of the typical NYSE share—those reactions will likely be reversed over time. Although the phrase "information cascade" had yet to be coined, Thaler and De Bondt effectively demonstrated how such overreaction offers a tremendous opportunity to make money, like the one that presented itself when investors overreacted to the potential for health care reform to harm Johnson & Johnson. When a company's stock price is dampened by pessimistic investors, odds are it will bounce back. Conversely, when a firm's share price is inflated by overly optimistic buyers, odds are it will fall back. It's an example, once again, of regression to the mean—the idea that extremes tend to revert back to something closer to the average. But it's also a reminder that the crowd is often wrong.

THE HERD IS SMALLER THAN YOU THINK

During a recent market plunge—when news reports mentioned that billions of dollars had been lost in a few days—a friend claimed that he could make a bundle if only he knew "where all that money was going." His logic: The money taken out of stocks had to be invested somewhere else. This common misconception is due largely to the fact that many people don't understand how stocks are priced and how the actions of a relatively small number of investors can seem like a stampede. Specifically, stock prices are set at the margins of shareholder ownership. If one hundred people own shares of Belsky & Gilovich Inc. stock worth $100 a share, the total market value of the company is $10,000 (100 times $100). Gary's mom decides to sell her share, but because there are no buyers at $100, she sells it to Tom's wife for $90. In the next day's paper, B&G Inc.'s stock price is listed at $90—the most recent sale price—so the company's market value is now $9,000 (100 times $90), a whopping 10 percent less than the day before. While some money has "left the market" —Gary's mom has $90 in her pocket—it's far less than the $1,000 loss in market value.

To be sure, we're not suggesting that you make investing decisions based solely on which stocks (or bonds or mutual funds) happen to be out of favor when you open the newspaper. Nor are we recommending that you sell your winners and hold on to your losers in the hope that regression to the mean will rescue you from your poor investment decisions. Such a strategy could be a recipe for disaster, inasmuch as the market is sometimes right on target. After all, Bre-X shares tumbled quickly once management's fraud was revealed, but that was hardly a reason to buy the company's stock.

Nonetheless, an entire school of investing is based on the premise that over short periods the market is often misguided but over the long run true value will win out. This school—called "value investing"—counts among its "graduates" some of the best investment minds in history, including Benjamin Graham, Warren Buffett, and John Neff. Over decades as investment managers and teachers—Graham was a legendary finance professor at Columbia University in New York City—these pros and others have demonstrated an uncanny knack for identifying companies that are out of favor with investors for any number of reasons, none of which has to do with their core business prospects. And over time those investors (including the noted mutual fund manager David Dreman) have been rewarded with market-beating investment returns. But even if you aren't confident enough (or foolish enough) to think that you can prospect for diamonds among lumps of coal, the lesson of this chapter is hardly diminished: If you insist on going along with the herd, you could very well find yourself heading straight for the slaughterhouse.

HOW TO THINK AND WHAT TO DO

WARNING SIGNS

You may be prone to following the herd if . . .

- you make investment decisions frequently.
- you invest in "hot" stocks or other popular investments.
- you sell investments because they're suddenly out of favor, not because your opinion of them has changed.
- you're likely to buy when stock prices are rising and sell when they are falling.
- you make spending and investment decisions based solely on the opinions of friends, colleagues, or financial advisers.
- your spending decisions are heavily influenced by which products, restaurants, or vacation spots are "in."

Life would be a whole lot simpler if we could tell you to ignore any and all investment trends and fads, but that would be a mistake.

Sometimes the crowd knows best. Millions of Americans have stampeded into the stock market over the past ten years or so, and following them would have been the right thing to do: a lot of money has been made by a lot of people as a result. Unfortunately, a lot more money might be in folks' pockets if they had managed to stick to a sound and simple investing strategy rather than following others blindly. Knowing when conventional wisdom is on target and when it is misguided is not easy, but the following suggestions should help you chart a safe and steady course of your own.

Hurry up and wait. When you're tempted to rush headlong into an investment trend, remember that financial fads are a lot like buses: there's no sense running after one, since another is certainly on its way. This is our way of saying that patience is paramount. Take the time and effort to thoroughly research any large-scale financial endeavor. Yes, there's a chance you might miss the boat. But there's as good a chance that you already have. If you're not sure, we urge you to remember the first rule of poker: If you look around the table and can't figure out who the sucker is, it's you. In any event, investment ideas that are worth their salt have staying power. A lot of people, nervous about taking their money out of banks and putting it into the stock market, missed most of the great run-up in stock prices during the 1980s. But many still made bucketloads of money when they finally started dipping their toes into the market at the beginning of this decade.

Avoid "hot" investments. That's particularly true with mutual funds, which relentlessly advertise their recent records as a way to lure investors. But funds often rack up their gains in short bursts of a few months or a year. By the time you sign up, the fun could be over. That's one reason we advise investing in index funds. But if you nonetheless choose to invest in actively managed mutual funds, you should concentrate on less trendy portfolios whose performance records are consistently good, not recently great.

Don't date your investments, marry them. We have already explained how some people have a problem letting go of their losing investment, which is true enough. But too many investors have the opposite problem: they view their relationship with a stock, bond, or mutual fund as nothing more serious than a Las Vegas quickie wedding, bouncing in and out as they chase one investing fad or another. That's why it's crucial that you assemble a portfolio of a half dozen to a dozen major investments (fewer if you invest in funds, more if you buy individual stocks) and stay with them for the long term—at least five years and preferably longer. Pay no more attention to the latest investment trend than you would to a waitress at Hooters or a dancer at Chippendales: nice to look at, but hardly someone you'd bring home to meet your mom. One way to help maintain your investing fidelity is to follow our next bit of advice.

Tune out the noise. During the early part of Gary's tenure at *Money,* the magazine would periodically poll Americans to see how savvy they were about investing. Among other questions, respondents were sometimes asked to choose among several numbers to find the one closest to the recent level of the benchmark Dow Jones Industrial Average. Increasingly, though, as the magazine's writers and editors began to understand more about behavioral economics, they began to understand that *not* knowing where the Dow was could just as easily be a sign of investing intelligence as investing ignorance. That's because the best investors often ignore the majority of what passes as important financial news these days.

We suggest you do the same. Unless you need your money quickly—in which case you should probably have your cash tucked away in safe money market accounts or funds—you're probably better off disregarding most financial news. Warren Buffett, chairman of Berkshire Hathaway and one of the wisest investors extant, explained this attitude in his company's 1993 annual report. Wrote Buffett: "After we buy a stock, consequently, we would not be disturbed if markets closed for a year or two. We don't need a daily quote on our 100% position in See's or H. H. Brown (companies wholly owned by Berkshire Hathaway) to validate our well-being. Why, then, should we need a quote on our 7% interest in Coke?"

This may seem reckless—ignoring most financial news, including changes in share prices—but it's not. Long-term investors need not concern themselves with yesterday's closing price or tomorrow's quarterly earnings reports. After all, the investor who bought Johnson & Johnson stock in 1990 and didn't look at it until recently would be very happy with the stock's appreciation and would be none the worse for having missed all the speculation about health care reform. It's a simplistic example, yes, but it's also true.

Finally, look for opportunities to be a contrarian. Again, we're not suggesting that you blindly invest in every loser stock out there. That would be silly and contrary to our belief that you should have most of your money invested in index funds. That said, to whatever extent you do choose to take an active approach to investing, you could do a lot worse than beginning your search for appropriate investments by focusing on those investments that the general public has turned its back on. As we've already mentioned, many of the most successful investors in history followed just such an approach.

Although this book is not an explicit "how to" investment guide, we'd be foolish if we didn't note that one of the smartest ways to evaluate stocks—if you're determined to do so—is to focus on those with below average price-to-earnings ratios, or P/Es.

A P/E is simply the ratio between a stock's price per share and its profits per share. It allows every company to be measured on an equal basis, regardless of size or business. So if Consolidated Steel is selling for $10 a share and has earnings per share of $1, the stock's price-to-earnings ratio is ten to one. Similarly, if Amalgamated Steel is selling for $100 a share but has earnings per share of $20, the stock's P/E is five to one. Two steel companies, one whose stock sells for $10 and one whose stock sells for $100. Yet the $100 stock is actually cheaper, a better bargain: for every $1 of Amalgamated profits, you must pay $5; $1 worth of Consolidated profits will cost you $10.

The reason investing in low P/E stocks can be considered a contrarian approach is this: P/Es reflect how much of a premium "the market" is willing to pay to own shares of a given company. The higher the P/E, the higher the premium—and, therefore, the more popular that stock is. Low P/E stocks, on the other hand, reflect diminished investor enthusiasm. By way of example, before Johnson & Johnson fell out of favor with investors as a result of concerns about health care reform, the company's average P/E in 1991 was 20.5. By 1994 J&J's P/E ratio had slipped to an average of 14.8. Investors were wrong in that case, and as a general rule, you can make a lot more money buying out-of-favor stocks with low P/Es than crowd-pleasing stocks that may be too highly priced and ripe for a fall.

Of course, it's not easy discerning worthwhile stocks with low P/Es from those that are justifiably ignored by most investors and thus valued at bargain-basement prices. One of the best "screens" to use when analyzing such out-of-favor companies is to invest only in those with sound balance sheets—in other words, not too much debt, a lot of cash in the bank, and profitable operations. But, frankly, it's probably not worth the effort. The real contrarian approach to investing is to rebel against your instinct for believing that you can make sense of balance sheets, stock reports, economic conditions, industry trends, and a dozen other factors that influence stock prices. As we will argue once more in the conclusion to this book, you'll likely be a lot richer if you cast your lot with a few mutual funds and forget about everything else but making regular contributions to them for the next ten, twenty, or thirty years.

CONCLUSION

NOW WHAT?

Life would be a lot simpler if we could summarize the ideas presented in this book with a set of prescriptive nuggets—"The Top Ten Mental Money Secrets" or "The Seven Habits of Financially Effective People." Unfortunately, there are no easy fixes for many of the issues we've touched upon. Change is often hard won. There's a reason, after all, why the majority of Weight Watchers members have been through the program before. Actually, the Weight Watchers analogy is particularly apt for the challenge you face in trying to give order to your financial decision-making processes. One of the difficult challenges in trying to change one's diet is that—unlike, say, smoking—you can't just stop cold turkey. You have to eat something. Similarly, you can't stop spending or investing or saving while you rethink the way you make financial decisions. You have to change course while in flight.

It is also difficult to alter many of the behavioral-economic habits we've discussed in this book because, although they cost you money, they reflect psychological tendencies that bring great benefits in other ways or in other areas. Almost all of these habits have a flip side that's beneficial, and it is these benefits that have made them so ingrained. As we have said earlier, the tendency to weigh losses more heavily than gains, for example, is doubtless a beneficial trait overall because an organism that cares too much about possible gains and too little about potential losses runs too great a risk of experiencing the kinds of losses that threaten its survival. The sunk cost fallacy is likewise connected to a predisposition with beneficial effects, a predisposition nicely captured by the injunction "Waste not, want not." A person who is too cavalier about previous expenditures might be too cavalier in other ways as well, and too wasteful. And as we discussed earlier, both the tendency to set up mental accounts and the predisposition to follow the herd can serve a person well. The barriers that exist between certain mental accounts can compensate for problems with self-control, and a tendency to look to others for guidance allows a person to take advantage of the information that others really do possess. It would be nice if we could take all of the benefits of these general tendencies and bear none of their costs, but it doesn't work that way. Not without a lot of effort, at any rate. What we're asking you to do is shed those parts of these general tendencies that exact a financial cost to you. But in doing so, you must recognize that you'll be fighting habits that are often rewarded in other ways and are thus held dear.

A second difficulty in summarizing and synthesizing the ideas in this book is one we hinted at in the introduction. Many behavioral-economic principles appear to conflict with one another, and appearances in this case are not deceiving. We can tell you in good conscience that people routinely overestimate their own abilities and knowledge, and we can follow that with an earnest discussion of the ways in which people blindly follow the actions of others. Both are true. So what should you do? Should you dismiss the crowd and always trust your instincts? Or should you recognize that you probably know a lot less than you think and put your faith and finances in the hands of others? The answer, not surprisingly, lies somewhere in the middle.

With these difficulties in mind, our next-to-last chapter approaches the concepts in this book from two angles. First, inside-out: the overarching ideas that inform behavioral-economic theory and how they affect your day-to-day and lifelong financial decisions. We've labeled this section "Principles to Ponder." Second, outside-in: things you can do now and the behavioral-economic reasons you might not already be doing them. We call this section "Steps to Take." Not very clever, we'll grant you, but to the point —as we hope this summation will be. In fact, we almost called the second section "Tom and Gary's Rebate Plan," because if nothing else, following these tips should return the cost of this book many times over.

PRINCIPLES TO PONDER

Every dollar spends the same. The term "mental accounting" is meant to describe the way people tend to treat money differently depending on where it comes from, where it's kept, or how it's spent. It can be a useful habit when it leads you to treat savings for college or retirement as sacred. But it can be dangerous when it causes you to spend money from some sources—such as gifts, bonuses, or tax refunds—more quickly than you might otherwise. Conversely, treating some money as *too* sacred—an inheritance, for example, or even long-term savings for a home, education, or retirement—can lead people to choose overly conservative investment strategies that avoid the ups and downs of the stock market but leave them exposed to the ravages of inflation. Whatever the case, how you label and treat different mental accounts is often the difference between amassing significant savings or finding your bank account wanting just when you need money most.

That's why it's important that you learn to view all money equally—salary, gifts, savings, even lottery winnings. One way to help this process along is to park "found" money in a savings or investment account before you decide what to do with it. The more time you have to think of money as savings—hard earned or otherwise—the less likely you'll be to spend it recklessly or impulsively. Conversely, to the extent that you *need* to have "mad money," you might consider putting a small percentage of your savings—say, 5 percent—in a special account designed for speculation or gambling or shopping sprees. If you can't kill the beast, tame it.

Losses hurt you more than gains please you. One of the central tenets of prospect theory—a bedrock principle of behavioral economics—is that people are "loss averse." The pain people feel from losing $100 is much greater than the pleasure they experience from gaining the same amount. This helps to explain why people behave inconsistently when taking risks. For example, the same person can act conservatively when protecting gains (by selling successful investments to guarantee the profits) but recklessly when seeking to avoid losses (by holding on to losing investments in the hope that they'll become profitable). Loss aversion causes some investors to sell *all* their investments during periods of unusual market turmoil. Although comforting in the short run, such efforts at timing the market don't work in the long run. This "asymmetry" between losses and gains can also work to your advantage. If you invest money through a payroll deduction plan, the savings is relatively painless because the reduction in your paycheck is experienced as a foregone gain (passing up a bigger check) rather than an outright loss (paying into savings "out of pocket").

Money that's spent is money that doesn't matter. The "sunk cost fallacy," one of the most common behavioral-economic mistakes, results in financial decisions that are based on previous investments or expenditures. Such a tendency is harmful for the simple reason that past mistakes shouldn't lead you to make future ones. The past is past, and what matters is what is likely to happen from now on. So a person who turns down an offer for a house because the bid is lower than the original purchase price may be following one blunder (paying too much in the first place) with another (not getting out while the getting is good). The sunk cost fallacy can sometimes be helpful—say, if you keep going to your gym because the annual membership dues were so expensive. But it can be harmful, too, helping to explain why people stay in unhappy careers or why individuals (or governments) continue to spend money on useless or wasteful projects. That's why it's important to remember that once money is spent it's generally gone. About the only choice a previous outlay should influence is the decision to ask for a refund.

It's all in the way you look at it. Another basic principle of behavioral-economic theory is that the way you frame decisions —particularly the way you "code" losses and gains—profoundly influences the choices you make. The same set of options might lead to a different decision depending on whether you view your choice as one of rejection or one of selection, or whether you view it as protecting a gain or avoiding a loss. That's why it's wise to view decisions from all sides—not just the pros and cons, but the ways in which a decision might be framed in your mind. This is especially useful for people who suffer from "decision paralysis," or an inability to make any choice at all. By turning the tables on the way you view problems, you can often clear away obstacles. For example, a person who can't decide among several different investment options in a retirement plan might assume that she already owns all or several of the available choices. The decision then becomes one of rejection ("Which investments am I uncomfortable owning?") rather than selection—and perhaps brings hidden considerations to light.

All numbers count, even if you don't like to count them. Throughout this book we've demonstrated the ways in which small numbers can add up to big costs. For example, the tendency to dismiss or discount small numbers as insignificant—what we call the "bigness bias"—can lead you to pay more than you need to for brokerage commissions and mutual fund expenses. And this can have a surprisingly deleterious effect on your investment returns over time. Similarly, the bigness bias and mental accounting allow people to "bury" small expenditures in bigger ones, while the "money illusion" leads people to ignore the harmful effects of inflation. Over time these incremental expenses and price hikes can be the difference between financial freedom and just scraping by.

You probably pay too much attention to things that matter too little. The tendency to weigh certain facts, figures, and events too heavily—to put too much stock in them—can be explained by a number of behavioral-economic principles. "Anchoring," for example, explains how people fixate on a specific dollar amount and base subsequent decisions on that figure, often mistakenly. People also tend to place too much emphasis on especially memorable or unusual events, not realizing that memory is much less reliable than they think. For example, many people remember the stock market crash of October 1987 and forget that stocks have offered the most consistent investment gains over time (and that, in fact, stocks rose slightly in 1987 as a whole). And many people become house poor by stretching to buy the largest home they can afford under the erroneous assumption that home prices are a better-than-average investment. In fact, although home prices soared for one brief period in the late 1970s, in most parts of the country they have roughly kept pace with inflation this century—and that's all.

Separately, a failure to fully grasp the role that chance plays in life leads many investors to be overly impressed with short-term success and other random or unusual occurrences. Thus, many investors pour money into mutual funds that have performed well in recent years under the often mistaken belief that the funds' success is the result of something other than dumb luck.

Your confidence is often misplaced. Nearly everyone falls prey, at one time or another, to an overestimation of their knowledge and abilities. This hubris, tough to admit but nonetheless very common, leads people into all manner of financial mischief. The most important is the belief that with a little knowledge or homework you can pick investments with better-than-average success. Overconfidence is a particularly seductive trap when people possess special information or personal experience—no matter how limited—that leads them to think their investment strategy is especially savvy. In reality, however, there is little reason for even the most sophisticated investor to believe that she can pick stocks—or mutual funds—better than the average man or woman on the street.

It's hard to admit mistakes. This sounds basic, but we're not talking about pride so much as we are the subconscious inclination people have to confirm what they already know or want to believe. This "confirmation bias" makes it hard for you to break patterns of thought and behavior because it leads you to find support for even the most questionable ideas and policies. Subsequently your ability to make sound spending and investment decisions is weakened because you don't evaluate relevant information with an even hand. Once again, then, it's important to temper your own self-confidence by sharing financial decisions with others—seeking not only specific advice, but critiques of your decision-making process.

The trend may not be your friend. The challenge in taking counsel from others is not to abandon completely your own instincts, common sense, and reason. "Herd investing" is just one example of the tendency to base decisions on the actions of others. In the long run, conventional wisdom is often on target—as it has been over the past twenty-five years in the trend away from fixed-income investments and toward stocks. In the short run, however, the vagaries of crowd behavior—particularly "information cascades," which result in very dramatic shifts in tastes and actions—frequently lead to costly overreactions and missed opportunities. That's why the most successful investors and spenders are those who view trends and fads with skepticism and caution.

You can know too much. Knowledge is power, but too much "illusory" information can be destructive. Studies have shown that investors who tune out the majority of financial news fare better than those who subject themselves to an endless stream of information, much of it meaningless. In part that's because the oblivious investor is unlikely to be swept up in information cascades or other herd investing tendencies. Similarly, the less frequently you check on your investments, the less likely you'll be to react emotionally to the natural ups and downs of the securities markets. For most investors, a yearly review of your portfolio is frequent enough.

STEPS TO TAKE

Raise your insurance deductible. The tendency to overweight memorable events and the failure to understand the odds of many potential hazards lead people to overestimate the likelihood that they'll have to file a claim against their life, health, and auto insurance. As a result, they buy insurance policies that include needlessly low deductibles and pay an excessively high price in the process. By hiking deductibles from, say, $100 or $250 to $500 or $1,000, you can often cut your premiums by 10 percent to 25 percent or more, enough to make up for the extra expense in the unlikely event that you'll have to file a claim.

Self-insure against small losses. The sensitivity to experiencing losses also leads people to take out insurance policies they do not need and that are not in their best interests. On average, insurance is a bad gamble for the consumer. Because insurance companies must pay agents and appraisers, employ a large clerical staff, and return a nice profit to shareholders, the amount they charge policyholders considerably exceeds the amount that policyholders get back in the form of claim reimbursements. Also, insurance companies have to allow for people in their "pool" who may be far more likely to file a claim than you, and that drives up your rates as well. As a result, you should have insurance only against losses that you cannot cover yourself. If your car was bought on credit, for example, by all means take out a collision and comprehensive policy to insure against damage. If you paid cash for it, however, you're better off just paying for liability coverage. If disaster strikes your car, you can have it repaired or buy another—either out of pocket (if yours are that deep) or with an auto loan. In the end, the odds are you'll come out ahead. Thus, whenever possible—that is, when you *can* cover the loss—be your own insurance company and pocket all the overhead costs that insurance companies would pass on to you.

Pay off credit card debt with emergency funds. This sounds reckless, but it's not, and it can save you big bucks. Here's the math: A lot of people have money stashed for a rainy day. By treating that money as untouchable, however, they typically keep it in ultrasafe bank accounts or money market accounts. At most, such savings earn about 5 percent a year, or $50 for every $1,000 invested. Yet many of these same people have credit card balances in the thousands—the typical family with plastic debt owes about $7,000—which costs them about 16 percent a year, or $160 for every grand. Simply by paying off your debt with emergency funds, you will save $110 for every $1,000 in borrowing. And don't worry about not having money for rainy days; credit card companies will be happy to lend you money if you're laid up, laid off, or just need a new bed to lay your head on.

Switch to index funds. This is one of the most important lessons of this book. A failure to understand the odds against beating the market—and overconfidence about their abilities to do so—causes many investors to pick their own stocks or actively managed mutual funds. In fact, the wiser course for most people is to pair their fortunes with those of the market averages by investing primarily in index funds. Index funds are portfolios that attempt to do no more than mirror the benchmark stock and bond averages in different investment categories. The idea is to guarantee that you will at least keep up with the typical investor—but, in fact, you'll likely do better than all those brave souls who think they can beat the law of averages. That's because actively managed portfolios are burdened by higher-than-necessary transaction and management expenses, not to mention faulty psychology and the law of averages. Index funds, as a rule, take much of the emotion out of investing. If you decide you want to take a more active hand in selecting investments, limit your exposure to your own psychological weaknesses by devoting no more than 25 percent of your assets to this approach.

Diversify your investments. Most investors who are still working should have the majority of their assets invested in the stock market, which has historically offered the best returns over time. Retirees also should invest in stocks with money that they'll need ten years or more down the road, while money they will need for current living expenses should be invested in safer securities such as money market instruments or short-term bonds.

But whatever the primary thrust of your portfolio allocation, diversifying at least partly among stocks (ideally stock index funds), bonds (bond index funds), money market funds, and real estate (real estate investment trusts) has two huge and related advantages. First, diversification allows you to benefit when a decline in the value of one asset is offset by a rise in the value of another. More important, the extent to which your overall portfolio shows steady growth rather than wild swings up and down could be the difference between you staying the course over the long run or pulling your money out of the markets when stocks hit a rough patch. You'll be less likely to succumb to loss aversion and other behavioral-economic tendencies that might lead you to do something drastic.

Review your assets. Diversification works only if you can view individual components of your portfolio in the context of your overall wealth. In order to do that you have to know what you are worth. That's why it's important to take stock of all your assets: retirement plans, real estate, savings accounts, art, and other collectibles. You need not know your worth to the penny, and you shouldn't undertake this exercise more than once every three months, but you should have some idea if your investments and other holdings balance out or leave you vulnerable.

Max out on retirement plans. Each year millions of Americans fail to contribute the maximum amount allowed to their retirement plan at work or don't contribute at all. If *you* don't max out, you are probably putting too great a value on what is yours—your salary today—and too low a value on what *could* be yours: free matching contributions from your employer and decades of tax-free investment gains. So contribute as much as you think you can to your 401(k), 403(b), or 457 plan at work and then contribute a little more!

Set up a payroll deduction plan. This is especially useful advice if loss aversion makes it difficult for you to save by writing a check to your savings or investment account. By funneling money directly from your paycheck into a special stock, bond, or money market mutual fund, small amounts of cash that you might have used for incidentals are mentally accounted for as sacred savings—and are less likely to be frittered away. Almost any fund company will help you set up such an automatic withdrawal plan.

Finally, keep track. If you're one of those lucky souls who can follow a budget, good for you. If not, one of the best ways to understand the behavioral-economic factors that affect the way you view and handle money—especially the ways in which the bigness bias leads you to pay too little attention to small numbers and amounts—is to track your spending. It sounds annoying, and it is. That's why we recommend that you try it for just one month, any month. If you can pull it off—writing down every single expenditure, big and small—you'll no doubt see patterns in your spending habits that will explain why you do not feel completely in control of your finances. And that's the first step in mastering your money.

POSTSCRIPT

PSYCHIC INCOME

There were numerous reasons that we decided to write this book, not least the money we hoped to earn for our efforts—money that, mindful of all these behavioral-economic tendencies, we would doubtless invest wisely. But we also believed that the ideas upon which this book rest—the principles of behavioral economics and decision science—deserved a hearing among the widest possible audience. Similarly, we wanted to pay homage to the many economists and psychologists whose creative and intellectual labors have for the most part gone unheralded among the general public—particularly Amos Tversky and Daniel Kahneman, true pioneers.

Mostly, though, we thought this book could help. We thought we could offer insights and advice that would aid you in dealing with one of the most complicated and critically important areas of life—your finances. Although some people are no doubt motivated by gathering wealth as an end unto itself, we believe that most folks think of money as a tool, a way to achieve goals and live a meaningful and enjoyable life. The paradox, of course, is that money is often one of the greatest causes of angst and frustration, a battle between idealistic aspirations and base realities. That's why we wanted to end this book with two pieces of advice, or two thoughts.

First, pick your fights. Even if you subscribe fully to everything we've explored in this book—even if you believe you now understand the causes of your financial missteps and the ways you can go about correcting them—the task ahead of you is daunting. And it's not always worth fighting. Trying to extract every last dime out of your financial decisions is likely to incur significant social and psychic costs. As you've no doubt noticed, not everyone likes a person who's obsessed with money. And even if everyone did, an insistence on always making *the* best financial decision in a given situation can lead to excessive worry and anxiety. Think of those annoying phone calls you receive at dinnertime asking if you'd like to switch your long-distance phone company. You might lower your phone bill a bit by listening to the full sales pitch, but do you really want to? Is it worth it? Not always. Nevertheless, it is our fervent hope that knowing about some of the behavioral-economic principles we've discussed will allow you to discard some bad habits and adopt a few good ones and thereby significantly improve your financial prospects.

With that in mind, you may find it easier (and more rewarding) if, rather than trying to incorporate all you've learned into your day-to-day decision-making process, you choose a couple of areas in which you'd like to effect change and attack those first. Certainly we'd like you to adopt all the advice we dispensed along the way that's relevant to your habits, especially the steps outlined in the previous chapter. But maybe a more realistic approach would be to consider the behaviors that are costing you the most money or anxiety and concentrate on them.

Second, go easy on yourself. However you choose to use the information and advice we've served up, be prepared to experience successes and failures. We make no promises about the ratio of one to the other, only that both will likely occur. But the extent to which you remain optimistic and patient—the extent to which you recognize that sea changes in behavior and attitude come infrequently and stubbornly—will largely determine your ability to persevere and experience real progress. Don't expect miracles or overnight transformations. Expect instead to learn some things about yourself, some things about the ways in which you make decisions in general and about money in particular. Like all knowledge, such awareness of self should translate into real wisdom and, with luck, wealth.

ACKNOWLEDGMENTS

We won't bore you with platitudes about how many people contributed to this book; we'll just bore you with a list of those people. Gary's thanks come first, then Tom's. Both of us, of course, are especially thankful to the people upon whose research this book stands.

G.B.:

To Elaine Pfefferblit, who was the first to suggest a book about behavioral economics. Events conspired to keep us from working together, but I'll always remember her prescience.

To Jane Dystel, everything you'd want in a literary agent: smart, loyal, and dogged. She also likes ideas, which helps.

To Fred Hills and Hilary Black at Simon & Schuster, who believed in what we had to say in this book and helped us say it even more clearly.

To Jason Zweig, my valued friend and colleague at *Money* and the best mutual fund writer in the country. Period. I asked Jason to read the manuscript for this book and have his way with it. He didn't disappoint.

To Clint Willis, my dear friend and former colleague at *Money.* Clint was the first to write about behavioral economics in the pages of *Money,* and he set the standard. I could do worse in life than follow in his footsteps. I also want to thank Kevin McKean, now an editor at Time Inc. New Media, and Frank Lalli, the former managing editor of *Money.* Kevin, who wrote about the work of Daniel Kahneman and Amos Tversky for *Discover* magazine, shepherded *Money's* early exploration of the topic. He was encouraged by Frank, who always had a nuanced understanding of the importance of psychology in personal finance.

To Russell Roberts, friend and fellow duffer. Russell taught me most of what I know about economics and more than a little bit about many other things. His comments on this manuscript were keen and kind, much like his friendship.

To Rance Crain and Mark Vittert, for their faith in my skills and in each other's judgment.

To my friends and colleagues who supported this project in substance or in spirit: Lisa and Jason Ablin, Lesley Alderman, Kim Aran, Meredith Berkman, Ephraim and Yedida Borow, Yaakov and Malke Borow, Brian and Tanya Clark, Therese and Dave Courtney, Harold and Rene Denlow, Caroline Donnelly, Beth Fenner, Malcolm Fitch, the Fredmans (Barry, Rena, Zev, Giela and Tamar), Carla Fried, Kay Friedman, Phyllis Furman, Lynn Goldner, Sarah Goldsmith, Caroline Haberfeld, Sue and Bengt Hagstrom, Jimmy and Lynn Harris, Bonnie Hilton-Green, Debbie Green, Irene and

Bruce Jacobs, Peter and Karen Keating, David Kingsley and Jena Cohen, Sid and Veevee Knopp, Joe and Jill Lazarov, Maggie Lear, Tyler Mathisen, Duff McDonald, Bobby Melnick, Phil and Mary Oppenheimer, Debi Pomerantz, Andy Regal, Patrick Reilly, Ron Reisler and Ilana Sultan, Cynthia Rigg and Abe Frajndlich, Saul Rosenberg, Suzy Ross, Whitney Rothschild, Deborah Schneider, Karen Schneider, Gloria Scoby, Beth and David Shaw, Ruth Simon, Michael Sivy, Jason Sklar, Randy Sklar, Frank Sommerfield, Ellen Stark, Mike Steinbaum and Deb Dubin, Patti Straus, Jay Susman, Teresa Tritch, Walter Updegrave, Ana Wilson, and Bear. If we're judged by the company we keep, I've gotten the better of the deal.

To Billie Pivnick, for her good counsel.

To my family, specifically my mom (Irene), my sisters (Barbara Belsky and Rhona Yolkut), my brothers (Howard and Jonathan), my brother-in-law (Larry Nudelman), my nephews and niece (Ari, Elly, Yirmi, Adir, Sam, and Zevvy), and my aunt and uncle (Annabelle and Kenny Chapel). You don't choose your family, but I would have.

To Mark and Linda Eisner, David and Jodi Kahn, and Dvora and David Reich. These folks, more than anyone, are responsible for my day-to-day sanity and overall optimism. I couldn't imagine life without them.

Finally, to my brother-in-law Myron Yolkut. I was six when Myron began dating my sister; he was sixteen. The first time I met him I jumped onto his back and, really, he's been carrying me there ever since. I hope this book doesn't make the load too much heavier.

T.G.:

To Amos Tversky and Daniel Kahneman, who have so greatly advanced what is known about the psychology of judgment and decision making and, in the process, have made the study of psychology so much more rewarding and so much more fun. To have had the privilege to work with both represents more good fortune than anyone could hope to have in one professional lifetime.

To Dick Thaler and Bob Frank, who gave me my education in economics and taught me that even that can be a playful experience. I am also indebted to both for their pivotal roles in creating the Cornell Center for Behavioral Economics and Decision Research. I have benefited enormously from the intellectual contributions of all of the center's many distinguished members: my dear friend Dennis Regan, Rob Bloomfield, Dave Dunning, Bob Gibbons, Alice Isen, Bob Libby, Vicki Medvec, Mark Nelson, Jeff Rachlinski, Jay Russo, Dave Sally, Bill Schulze, and Kathleen Valley.

To Karen Dashiff Gilovich. The only reason I can have the chutzpah to write about judgment and decision making is that the most important decision of my life was, without doubt, the wisest. But of course it was not driven by wisdom, and it was also the easiest I've ever made.

To the National Institute of Mental Health and the National Science Foundation for supporting my research.

ABOUT THE AUTHORS

Award-winning journalist **Gary Belsky** was a writer at *Money* magazine from 1991 through 1998, covering all aspects of personal finance. From 1994 through 1998 he was a regular weekly commentator on CNN's *Your Money* personal finance show and a frequent contributor to ABC's *Good Morning America.* Currently a senior editor at *ESPN The Magazine,* Belsky graduated from the University of Missouri in his hometown of St. Louis in 1983 with a BA in political science and speech communication. Before joining *Money* magazine, he was a reporter for *Crain's New York Business* and the *St. Louis Business Journal.* In 1990, Belsky won the Gerald Loeb Award for Distinguished Business and Financial Journalism, the most prestigious award given to business or personal finance reporters and writers. He lives in New York City.

Thomas Gilovich is a professor of psychology at Cornell University in Ithaca, N.Y. A native Californian, Gilovich received his BA from the University of California in 1976 and his Ph.D. from Stanford University in 1981. An award-winning teacher, he lectures both nationally and internationally on everyday reasoning and decision making, and on the fallibility of human judgment. His research on these and other topics has been published in the *Journal of Personality and Social Psychology, Psychological Review,* and *Cognitive Psychology,* among many other academic journals and popular magazines. His research is summarized in his book *How We Know What Isn't So.* He lives with his wife and two daughters in Ithaca.